❧ A Woman's Wit & Whimsy ❧

THE NEW ENGLAND WOMEN'S DIARIES SERIES
Co-published by the Massachusetts Historical Society

NEW YEAR IN CUBA
Mary Gardner Lowell's Travel Diary, 1831–1832
Edited by Karen Robert

A WOMAN'S WIT & WHIMSY
The 1833 Diary of Anna Cabot Lowell Quincy
Edited by Beverly Palmer

A WOMAN'S WIT & WHIMSY

THE NEW ENGLAND WOMEN'S DIARIES SERIES

The 1833 Diary of Anna Cabot Lowell Quincy

Edited by BEVERLY WILSON PALMER

Massachusetts Historical Society

Northeastern University Press

Boston

Garden pond.
Mt Auburn.

NORTHEASTERN UNIVERSITY PRESS

Copyright 2003 by the Massachusetts Historical Society and Northeastern University Press

Library of Congress Cataloging-in-Publication Data

Waterston, Anna Cabot Lowell Quincy, 1812–1899.
A woman's wit and whimsy : the 1833 diary of Anna Cabot Lowell Quincy /
edited by Beverly Wilson Palmer.
p. cm. — (The New England women's diaries series)
Includes bibliograpical references and index.
ISBN 1-55553-575-5 (acid-free paper) —
ISBN 1-55553-574-7 (pbk. : acid-free paper)
1. Waterston, Anna Cabot Lowell Quincy, 1812–1899—Diaries. 2. Women—
Massachusetts—Boston—Diaries. 3. Poets, American—19th century—Diaries.
4. Boston (Mass.)—Social life and customs. 5. Upper class—Massachusetts—
Boston. 6. Boston (Mass.)—Biography. 7. Quincy family.
I. Palmer, Beverly Wilson, 1936– II. Title. III. Series.
PS3157.W33Z477 2003
818'.403—dc21   2003008328

Book design and typography in Quadraat by Christopher Kuntze.
Printed and bound by Sheridan Books, Ann Arbor, Michigan.
The paper is House Natural Hi-Bulk, an acid-free stock.

MANUFACTURED IN THE UNITED STATES OF AMERICA

07 06 05 04 03   5 4 3 2 1

CONTENTS

THE DIARY

ILLUSTRATIONS

Preface ❧ The New England Women's Diaries Series

I walked into the Massachusetts Historical Society for the first time in the early 1970s. When I told the woman at the desk that I wanted to write about women in colonial New England, she said, "Good luck. You won't find much." Neither at the MHS nor at any of the other archives I visited were there any guides to women's papers. My only recourse was to sift through various collections of family papers, page by page, looking for material relevant to my project.

All that has changed. One of the consequences of the renaissance in women's history over the past thirty years is that archives all over the United States now have finding aids to women's papers. In the process of preparing one such guide, Ondine LeBlanc decided that the time had come to share with a larger public the extraordinary collection of women's diaries at the Massachusetts Historical Society. More than two hundred diaries, ranging from the colonial period to the late twentieth century, document an astonishing range of female activity, from ocean travel to spiritual exploration. The authors include farmwives, teachers, urban activists, household servants, literati. Their stories encompass a panorama of social experience, from the frontlines of World War I to the plantations of nineteenth-century Cuba.

The forms of the diaries also vary. Some are taciturn, others expansive. Some focus on interior life, others on daily labor. Some are as steady as a clock or an almanac; others episodic, ebbing and flowing with the tides of event or emotion. Some are travel journals filled with local color and ethnographic observation. Others, originating as personal communications to a trusted friend, belong to that familiar mixed genre the "letter journal." Whatever the form, they fit the classic definition of the diary as a personal account of daily (if not every day) experience.

The New England Women's Diaries Series is a joint venture of the Massachusetts Historical Society and Northeastern University Press. Our intended audience is the proverbial "general reader." As a consequence, we have chosen diaries for their intrinsic interest as well as for their value as historical sources. Introductions, written by scholars with expertise in the period, place, or general subject matter of the diaries, provide rich contextual introductions but keep scholarly apparatus to a minimum. Wherever possible, we present each diary in its entirety.

The words "diary" and "journal" are both rooted in the notion of the daily unfolding of events human or heavenly. Thus, in Old French, variations on the word "journal" could connote both the movement of the sun across the sky and the amount of land a team of oxen could plough in a day. The reader of a diary sees a life unfold as it happens, bit by bit, with all the unrealized plots, dead ends, and confusions of ordinary life. There is predictability—the sun comes up, the sun goes down, fields are planted, journeys begun and ended, sentences move across the page, persons are born, grow old or fall ill, and die. Yet diaries, like life, are filled with the suspense of unrealized aspiration. What new joy or terror lies just around the corner? A good diary provides many of the satisfactions of a good novel. It lets the reader inside another person's life, offering the intimacy of a vicarious friendship. Yet because diaries, unlike novels, develop incrementally, the stories are always cluttered with incidentals and never complete. Sometimes events come to a satisfying resolution; more often they sputter to an end in half-finished sentences on a still empty page. Introductions, footnotes, maps, photographs, and occasional selections from other texts can help explain "what happened," but these devices can never provide the resolution—or the artifice of fiction.

A good diary keeps its secrets. That is its challenge and its charm.

Laurel Thatcher Ulrich
Series Editor

ACKNOWLEDGMENTS

No documentary edition results from a single person's efforts. The Anna Quincy diary is no exception, for many people have contributed to this publication. Ondine LeBlanc, Associate Editor of Publications at the Massachusetts Historical Society, helped me select this remarkable diary from the Society's collections, and then ably advised me as my editing of it proceeded. Both Ondine and Elizabeth Swayze, Acquisitions Editor, Women's Studies, of Northeastern University Press, have provided valuable feedback on transcription policies and drafts of the introductory material. Elizabeth has expertly guided me through the publication sequence. I thank Laurel Thatcher Ulrich, Phillips Professor of Early American History at Harvard University, and Women's Diary Series Editor, for helping me see additional implications in Anna's work and for her wise words of encouragement. Comments on the introduction from both Laurel and an anonymous reader for Northeastern were enormously useful as I completed work on the diary.

Aiding me in my research at the Massachusetts Historical Society have been Nicholas Graham, Reference Librarian, Carrie Foley, former Assistant Reference Librarian, and Kate DuBose, Reading Room Supervisor, all of whom cheerfully and competently ferreted out pertinent material from the Society's archives. Jean Powers, formerly Editorial Assistant for Publications at the Society, assisted in the proofreading of a good part of my transcription of the document.

At the Harvard University Archives, Brian A. Sullivan, Reference Archivist, was always ready to assist me as I searched through the University's records for temporary members of the Harvard community and I appreciate both his enthusiasm for the project and knowledge of nineteenth-century Harvard University life. Additionally, I wish to thank Robin McElhenry at the University Archives as well as Sally Hild at the Cambridge Historical Society. Kathleen Rawlins at the Cambridge Historical Commission located two illustrations for the volume. Elizabeth Dunn, Research Services Librarian, and her colleagues at the Rare Book, Manuscript, and Special Collections Library at Duke University assisted me with research in their extensive resources there.

In California, Pomona College generously provided computer assistance and several research grants. Edward Copeland, emeritus professor of English at Pomona College, identified several of Anna Quincy's puzzling

Acknowledgments

references. Kristin Fossum in the associate dean's office provided helpful comments on a final draft of the introduction.

Finally, my husband, Hans C. Palmer, professor of economics at Pomona College, has supported my work on the diary in every phase from proofreading my transcription to critiquing the introductory essays. Without his advice the project could not have been completed.

Although these advisors and assistants have been crucial to the completion of this edition, any faults that remain in the published work are my own.

Beverly Wilson Palmer

❦ A Woman's Wit & Whimsy ❧

Conversation turned upon the various characters we saw in Cambridge
& the amusement it was to observe the difference of characters— "Yes"
said I, "almost every visitor is a complete contrast to the preceeding—"
"Ladies I congratulate you"—said Mr S. rising— "Your next visitor will
I hope be a complete contrast to yr. Last"—& vanished. The extreme
oddity of his manner entirely deprived us of all power of answering & as
soon as he was gone, we fell back, & laughed heartily (10 August 1833).

In March 1833 twenty-year-old Anna Quincy started a diary. In part it served
as her record of the Quincy family's social activities while Anna's two sisters traveled to the southern United States. Yet this diary also became a
storehouse of Anna's satirical views of the young men of Cambridge and
Boston. With topics ranging from Harvard University soirées to Boston
cotillions, Anna's journal entries present a trenchant and amused account
of the privileged environment that she enjoyed. The opening sentence of
Jane Austen's novel *Emma* could well be a portrait of this young woman:
"handsome, clever, and rich, with a comfortable home and happy disposi-
tion, [she] seemed to unite some of the best blessings of existence; and had
lived nearly twenty one years in the world with very little to distress or
vex her."

No writer influenced Anna Quincy more deeply than Austen. Describing
days filled with walking, drawing, reading, paying calls to family and
friends, and receiving visitors, Anna tried to recreate in her journal a society similar to that in Austen's novels.[1] In chapter 3 of *Northanger Abbey* Henry
Tilney asks Catherine Morland, "How are the civilities and compliments of
every day to be related as they ought to be unless noted down every evening
in a journal?" As depicted in her diary, Anna's and her sisters' lives resemble that of Emma Woodhouse, as well as those of Elizabeth and Jane Bennet in *Pride and Prejudice*, or Elinor and Marianne Dashwood in *Sense and
Sensibility*, where the rites of courtship predominate, appearances are both
significant and deceiving, and callow young men vie for a spirited woman's
attention.

Anna Cabot Lowell Quincy descended from a long line of distinguished
and wealthy figures. Her great-grandfather Josiah Quincy had amassed a
fortune from shipbuilding and trade in the eighteenth century. His son and

Anna's grandfather, Josiah Quincy Jr., became a prominent lawyer and died at sea while returning from a mission on behalf of the colonists protesting British rule. Anna's household was headed by her father, also named Josiah Quincy, who had served in the U.S. Congress for eight years and been mayor of Boston for five. Defeated for another mayoral term in 1828, he became president of Harvard University the following year, the first non-clergyman in the post.

Anna's middle names testify to the Quincy family's close ties to Boston's elite, for her mother chose to name her youngest daughter in memory of her close friend Anna Cabot Lowell, daughter of Judge John Lowell and niece of U.S. senator George Cabot. Anna's mother, Eliza Morton Quincy, had also known privilege. A native of New York City, where her father had been a merchant, Eliza Morton married Josiah Quincy in 1797 and bore him nine children, of whom seven lived to be adults. Besides raising these children, Eliza readily assumed the social responsibilities as wife of the mayor of Boston and later president of Harvard. In a reflection written in April 1886, when Anna was a married woman in her seventies, she recalled her mother's "graceful, cordial manners"; "no one liked society better than my mother." Eliza Morton Quincy had gladly assumed the role of helpmeet to a distinguished civic leader. According to her daughter, Eliza Quincy was "singularly adapted both for domestic and public life" and an excellent hostess.[2]

The youngest of five daughters and two sons, Anna knew the security of an eminent family. She was christened at the Federal Street Church by its renowned pastor, the theologian William Ellery Channing. According to the historian Edward Pessen's tallies, the Quincy family's wealth at the time placed them in the $100,000–$250,000 bracket, a remarkable figure considering that in 1833 Anna's father earned an annual salary of slightly over two thousand dollars as president of Harvard.[3]

In her sketch of her childhood and early years, Anna looked back on the "handsome" houses in which she lived. A home surrounded by spacious grounds on Pearl Street, the site of Anna's birth, afforded a fine view of the Boston harbor. The family soon moved to Summer Street, considered one of the most elegant in Boston. But the real home, the site of Anna's most precious childhood memories, was the family house in Quincy, eight miles from Boston. Built in 1770 by her great-grandfather the shipbuilder, this residence served as the summer home for the Quincys throughout Anna's long life. The estate of Josiah Quincy's aunt Sarah Quincy Dowse ("Aunt

Dowse"), in Dedham on the banks of the Charles River, offered yet another family retreat.[4] Thus Boston and environs that Anna knew were devoid of poverty, dirt, and slums.

Anna's large and active family emerge in her diary as an affectionate, close-knit group. Four years younger than her nearest sibling, Edmund, and six years younger than her sister Margaret, Anna, often called Nannie, was "naturally the pet and spoiled child of the family." With four older sisters and a mother whom she greatly admired, Anna had not only frequent companions but also compelling role models. Margaret's marriage in 1826, when Anna was just entering her teens, became the first "break in the family circle," yet, as the diary indicates, the sisters continued to share many activities.[5] A year after Margaret's marriage, their brother Josiah married Mary Jane Miller, who bore two nephews, "Josy" and Sam. In Anna's diary her brother Edmund courts his fiancée, Lucilla Parker, whom he will marry in the fall. None of the three other sisters married, and in 1833, when we enter Anna's world, they all live at home: Susan at thirty-five, Abigail at thirty, and Sophia at twenty-eight. The two brothers practice law in Boston and the father presides over Harvard. Although she freely criticizes male foibles, Anna Quincy accepts her place in a society run by men. Clearly they govern her family's professional and economic life, their activities rarely impinging on Anna's.

When she was fifteen, Anna attended a French school on Chesnut (as it was spelled in the 1830s) Street for only one year. With typical modesty she wrote that this sole exposure to formal education "opened a new world to me—too new, I fear, and too full of various interruptions for so undisciplined a mind to gain all that it might have gained from the opportunity offered." Most upper-class girls in Boston had more schooling outside the home than did Anna. Young women between fifteen and twenty were expected to master French, Italian, and perhaps a little Latin, in order to read the literature of France and Italy. They were advised to study Plutarch's lives and have some knowledge of geography. Yet, according to the *Young Lady's Own Book*, education for young women should be "strictly feminine," without emphasis on "professional knowledge." Female education should instill certain values, producing women with "amiability, intelligence, and an absence of affectation." An educated woman should never "obtrude her knowledge."[6]

No doubt keenly aware of these goals, Anna's parents nevertheless schooled their daughters at home. This departure from conventional upbringing may have resulted from Josiah Quincy's dislike of public education for females. As mayor of Boston, he had abolished the girls' high school in 1828, an unpopular decision attacked in the press as elitist. At home then, under the tutelage of their mother, the daughters read literary classics by William Shakespeare, John Milton, and Sir Walter Scott. Anna fondly recalled the mornings when Eliza read aloud to them from these works. In taking charge of the girls' education, Anna's mother emphasized "love of home, love of nature, and love of reading." Anna wrote later that "it being before the days of higher education [for women] my brain . . . was not ruined by overwork." Yet the numerous quotations in her journal from Shakespeare, Lord Byron, and Alexander Pope attest to a solid literary background. Moreover, in 1831 and 1837 Anna filled two volumes, known as commonplace books, with the nature poetry of American poets such as Fitz-Greene Halleck and his contemporaries. Dedicated to her sister Margaret, these journals also include Anna's drawings and verse that is likely her own.[7]

When Anna was sixteen, her father assumed the Harvard presidency, an appointment that, she later noted, "caused a great change in the family arrangements." In May 1829 the family moved across the Charles River to Wadsworth House in Cambridge, a residence affording a large garden and an "ample stable" surrounded by "wide grounds." Anna remembered her father's "noble appearance in the presidential robes" when he was inaugurated on 2 June 1829 as the fifteenth president in a ceremony attended by Governor Levi Lincoln and other dignitaries.[8]

Josiah Quincy provided his family with its income and its standing in society, yet he remains a shadowy figure in his youngest daughter's diary. He squires her to church, escorts the family to a Boston party, and brings sad news of the deaths of John Ashmun and George Davis. Only during the presidential visit of Andrew Jackson in June does Anna portray her father as the Harvard president, as he arranges the ceremonies to honor the U.S. president and deals with the uncertainties accompanying Jackson's visit (see the introduction to Chapter 4). Josiah represents a life far removed from Anna's. Her connection to Harvard comes only through the men, young and old, who visit the family's "humble bower" on the university grounds.

Besides taking her daughters' education in hand, Eliza instilled in them proper behavior for young unmarried ladies. They were not to step outside the circumscribed roles society had established for them. Though they were probably delighted that women could now visit the Boston Athenaeum "unattended by a gentleman," the Quincy women would never have exhibited any protests to bring about that privilege. Anna learned to receive callers graciously, avoid excessive physical contact with young gentlemen, and always travel in public with a companion. She followed her mother's precept that women should not "emulate men in their vocations" and should remain "merely women."[9]

In the diary, as she follows contemporary customs for some unmarried women, Anna does not participate in the "exhibition" of the waltzers at John Welles's cotillion (22 March). She refuses to walk down State Street "with out a gentleman" (23 July). After a luncheon for Edmund and two of his male friends, she obligingly departs, according to the custom of the day (30 March). She also acquiesces when temporarily forbidden to view the scantily clad models of Canova statues at a Boston exhibition (2 August). In her journal then, Anna expresses few reservations, except in mildly ironic statements, about her limited role as a mere female.

Neither her education nor her lessons in deportment, however, stifled her independent personality. In the diary's description of her encounters with men, Anna portrays herself as far from docile. The etiquette books of the day stressed that young women should strive to be pure and refined in order to serve as edifying influences on the young men of their acquaintance. Since the sexes were "manifestly intended for different spheres," women's upbringing required "quiet training"; they should look to men, clearly their "superior," for guidance. A woman "knows she is the weaker vessel . . . her weakness is an attraction, not a blemish."[10] These descriptions hardly apply to the young woman who on 26 June clambers merrily about the *Columbus* with two naval officers (albeit with Mrs. Minot as chaperone) or to the one who acidly comments on the "Cambridge worthies." Amid the staid society surrounding her, Anna found a release for her high spirits in the diary, a place where she could exaggerate and satirize her social world.

In her frequent descriptions of her forays into society, old and young men abound. Anna dances and dines with many of the young men, often three or four in a single evening, before she is "armed out" by one of them at the evening's close. Generally she treats with respect the older men, friends of her father's or Harvard professors, saving her dismissive comments for undergraduates such as Thomas Rutledge ("silly child") or the law student Thomas Church ("boobyish & disagreeable"). Of the young men she treats positively, many appear to be simply companions, such as Tom Dwight, Tom Davis, and the Cleveland brothers, Horace and Henry, friends of Edmund's and therefore almost like older brothers. She expresses admiration for the law student William Chaplain ("Leicester"), the young Boston merchant Robert Storer, and the naval officer Henry Davis, yet the diary does not indicate romantic attraction. "A man of sense is not so easily found," she notes on 1 May.

In her 10 April entry prompted by the sudden departure of the law student Francis Vinton, Anna mockingly laments men's fecklessness: "'I'll keep my heart another day', in the hope that the shadow of chivalry—politeness, yet adorns the noble Leicester— Should he too prove that 'friendships balmy words but feign' we shall be forced to exclaim with Sir Peter Teasle 'This is a—wicked world we live in, and the fewer we praise in it the better.'—" At this stage of her life, Anna regards men generally as targets for her pen rather than potential suitors. She prefers to entertain her sisters with descriptions of the "ridiculous & the unmeaning" behavior of the young men like Joseph ("Shocco") Jones and Francis Vinton (21 March).

Convention forbade laughter in public; young ladies should also refrain from exaggeration or ridicule. In *The Young Lady's Friend*, Eliza Farrar, the wife of a Harvard professor of mathematics, wrote, "The love of ridicule grows by indulgence, till it destroys the power of discrimination, lessens the sensibility to others' pain . . . and gives a general taint of coarseness to the whole character."[11] If Farrar ever imparted such advice to Anna, it went unheeded. Although she usually adheres to societal customs in public, privately Anna ignores them. At home in their own parlor or bedroom, she and her sisters regularly laugh at the foibles of the young males in Cambridge and Boston and the ridiculous situations that ensue. Furthermore, the diary becomes the place where she engages in the ridicule so frowned upon by the arbiters of good behavior.

With the close of this diary, the sprightly character in it also disappeared. In her later letters and published writings, there emerges a more refined, conventional woman than the Anna of the diary. The writings of the married Anna Quincy Waterston lack the clever, barbed commentary of the twenty-one-year-old diarist. Her 1886 autobiographical sketch, although valuable for its details, conveys only warm and nostalgic words about her youth. Missing is the intense vibrancy of the 1833 document, in which Anna melodramatically mourns the engagement of Stephen Salisbury ("nothing else, can equal the grandeur of being Countess of Salisbury & at the head

8

of the great Worcester estate," 1 May) or describes her sister and herself who, "arrayed fantastically in dressing gowns" at the top of the stairs in Wadsworth House, just miss being spotted by Henry Cleveland: "He probably would have taken us for some Grecian Statues suddenly endowed with life" (10 June). What happened to this witty young woman?

None of the young men mentioned in the diary became Anna Quincy's husband. Unfortunately, no record has apparently survived of the courtship of Robert Cassie Waterston and Anna Quincy. They became engaged in January 1839, an event, according to Anna's brother Edmund, "which gives much satisfaction to all concerned & the more, the more is seen of the young man & his family." In November 1839 the twenty-seven-year-old Robert Waterston was ordained as a Unitarian minister. Anna married him five months later, on 21 April 1840, at the age of twenty-seven. The ceremony, conducted by Henry Ware Jr., took place at Wadsworth House, and a "stand-up supper was served in the left hand drawing room" afterward. Besides the family, those attending whom Anna mentions in her 1833 diary were the Minot, Guild, and Welles families.[12]

Robert C. Waterston was a bookish, undistinguished man (if a tribute to him by Anna's nephew is to be believed), one who would be remembered as "a lover of the good and the beautiful, and as a patient explorer of a little segment in the vast circle of human interests."[13] One wishes that this suitor (who, significantly, is not mentioned in her autobiographical sketch) had been subjected to Anna's pen. The few surviving letters between the couple after their marriage contain only the conventional expressions of affection. Did Robert Waterston have the appeal of a Robert Storer, "so truly excellent & sensible in his appearance & conversation, & so gentlemanly in his manner" (30 April)? Was he, like the attentive William Chaplain, "all elegance" (31 March)?

Anna's husband was the son of a wealthy Boston merchant. He attended the Harvard Divinity School in 1836–37 but did not receive a degree. As a Unitarian missionary to the poor, he first ministered from the Pitts Street Chapel in Boston. From 1846 to 1852 he served the Church of the Saviour in Boston, until it was forced to close because of mounting debts and a decreasing congregation. Thereafter Robert Waterston retired to a life of occasional preaching, study of literature, and involvement in civil affairs. He published numerous tracts on Christian worship, education, and moral culture, as well as discourses on prominent Bostonians. Known for his verbose enthusiasm, he expressed progressive and enlightened views on immigration and the causes of poverty. But on religious matters he was conservative.[14] A congenial traveling companion, Robert Waterston apparently shared, and perhaps encouraged, his wife's scholarly pursuits.

Both Anna and Robert Waterston held ardent antislavery opinions, not always a popular stand in antebellum New England. No doubt influenced by Edmund, an active Garrisonian abolitionist, Anna praised the speeches of her friend Senator Charles Sumner and encouraged his antislavery efforts. While traveling extensively in Europe in 1856–57 with their daughter, Helen, the Waterstons met antislavery leaders such as the Irish Quaker Richard D. Webb in Dublin and Elizabeth Pease Nichol in Glasgow. In a letter of 29 August 1856 to Edmund, Anna includes news of British abolitionists and concern over the violence in the United States over slavery. "I have little hope of the so called free states," she concludes. Her Civil War poem "On Seeing the Flag Again Floating Over Chester Square" indicates her strong Northern sympathies at a time when most of her state had come to rally around the antislavery cause:

> Above our homes a storm had burst,
> And the tall staff was rent in twain;
> But high above the lightning, soared
> The Eagle through the fire and rain;
> True omen of that lightning flash,
> Rending the staff where Slavery clings,
> Which leaves our Eagle soaring yet
> Above us with her unclipt wings.
> Beneath a clearer sky shall float
> Our banner on the north-wind free,
> And the whole earth shall hail with joy
> The stainless flag of Liberty.[15]

Anna and Robert lost both their children before adulthood. A son, Robert, died at age one in 1846, and Helen died at seventeen in Naples on 25 July 1858, after a sudden decline and illness attributed to a weak heart. The parents' stoicism over the final illness and loss of their remaining child is poignantly reflected in the 1858 volume that Robert presented to his wife with its inclusion of poems by William Cullen Bryant and William Wordsworth, as well as scripture, hymns, and meditations on death. Anna's letters after Helen's death indicate her devastation; she wrote Anna Hazard Ward: "Helen was so much to us—and to me was more like a sister than a child. I was very dependant upon her for my daily life & comfort— Hers was a far more calm and reliable nature than mine."[16]

From the 1860s on, from their home in Chester Square in Boston, Anna immersed herself in concerns over her nieces and nephews, and in the professions of other young women. She closely followed the career of a now obscure opera singer, Adelaide Phillipps (1833–82), of whom she wrote a biography in 1883. She took a similar interest in the career of another young woman, Kate Field (1838–96), a writer and lecturer.[17] Surviving documents indicate that the saucy diary writer thus became an upper-class woman occupied with her family, friends, civic affairs, and her writing.

Anna's early penchant for literary expression bore fruit with a number of later publications. In 1863 she published *Verses* along with "Together," a tribute to the Civil War officer Robert Gould Shaw, who died leading African American troops in the July 1863 attack on Fort Wagner, South Carolina. In the 1860s the *Atlantic Monthly* published her articles "The Visible and Invisible in Libraries" (on the thrilling treasures to be found in the Oxford and Cambridge university libraries), "Annesley Hall and Newstead Abbey," and "Woman's Work in the Middle Ages."[18]

In the last article Waterston describes the needlework, weaving, and lace that medieval women produced. Anna argues that "as far as they were faithful to the duties appointed to them [these women] elevated their sex to a higher and nobler position." In supervising domestic work in "baronial halls" and castles, women assumed considerable responsibility: they "must have worked there with brain and fingers." Even from the earliest times, Anna shows, some women read widely and deeply enough that "conversation at the dinner-tables of the fifth century might be quite as edifying as at those of the nineteenth." She concludes that "a wider sphere is now accorded, and a deeper responsibility devolves upon woman to fill it wisely and well."[19]

In the early 1870s Anna Waterston helped to found the Woman's Education Association, an organization formed to enlighten and stimulate upper-class women through a series of lectures given by Harvard professors and other learned men. The WEA also sought to "improve" the education of female teachers so that they could be better equipped morally and intellectually to deal with the current inequitable system. The organization hoped ultimately to enroll some women, presumably in an adjunct capacity, at Harvard, as well as to place women on local school boards. Although the records suggest that Anna was not one of the WEA's leaders, she did sign the call for its initial meeting. For two years she served on the Committee on Moral and Physical Education, but after 1873 her name disappears from the WEA's minutes.[20]

Robert Waterston died in February 1893, at age eighty-one. Anna then considered herself a true survivor, for by the end of that year all her siblings had died. A birthday tribute to her old friend Dr. Oliver Wendell Holmes later that year conveys her fond recollections of her youth: "Few of us are left, but we stand together. You have so many letters from friends, I only write mine, because I was once Anna Quincy and one of the girls of 1829."[21]

Anna Cabot Lowell Quincy Waterston ends her autobiographical sketch with a description of her first ball, when she was seventeen. She recalls her dress—white silk lace over white satin—and the compliment she received from a Boston society matron. She closes the reflection with this nostalgic comment: "Every other trace of the ball has disappeared from my memory, but the gratification of being noticed by Mrs. Derby was too great not to be remembered. The graceful, beautiful, matron and the blooming young girl have alike vanished."[22]

Yet the blooming young girl survives through her diary.

Most women's journals in the nineteenth century reflect the constricted worlds they inhabited. Their diaries vary both in type and in motive (frequently overlapping) for keeping them. Some wanted simply to record passing events: meals cooked, callers who visited, and perhaps the more significant births, marriages, and deaths. Others kept diaries only in special situations, most often on a trip, as did Lucretia Coffin Mott when she went to the British Isles in 1840. Anna Quincy herself kept a travel diary when she went to upstate New York in 1834. Still others used their diaries for introspection, an examination of their emotions and thoughts, reactions to troubling or pleasing events in life.[23]

Anna's diary initially served an informing purpose, a purpose that governed her mode of expression. She addressed the first two volumes, comprising the months of March through mid-June, to "my dear Margy," her older sister Margaret Greene, who had departed with another sister, Abigail, on a trip to New York and points south. Here Anna seeks to preserve for Margy and Abby the family's activities during the sisters' absence. The occasional references and terminology (she addresses Margy as "my dear Flamabella," for example) that are mysterious to an outsider remind us that this writing is indeed private. Perhaps consciously, Anna adopts some of Margaret's own diary language and frequent use of quotations.[24] Similar though it may be in language, however, Margaret's diary lacks Anna's witty portraits.

Indicating her continued proclivity for creative expression, Anna continued the diary after Margaret's return. (Parts of volume 3 may have been written for her sisters Susan and Sophia, who with their father traveled to Niagara Falls from 24 July to 15 August 1833.) Anna's verve makes clear that she enjoyed writing for herself as much as, if not more than, for any wide audience. And after the entries had been written, Anna returned to them; on occasion she and her sisters read "that most profitable volume" aloud to each other (see, for example, the entry for 29 May). The corrections and biographical updates she added years later indicate her regard for the 1833 journal. Yet apart from the 1834 travel diary, apparently Anna kept no other diary.

Although many entries consist of days when "nothing happened" or she "stayed home all day," most of the time Anna seizes upon a social event to demonstrate her ability to describe and satirize. She aims to entertain. Thus as both participant and observer, she emphasizes the ridiculous (or, to use one of her favorite words, "absurd") aspects of an occasion. Such self-conscious analysis of both the event and her role in it typifies Anna's writing. Indeed, she uses sprightly and irreverent descriptions laced with humor to portray herself in awkward or odd situations. For example, in the 29 March entry she playfully relates how, when attempting to repair a bit of trim on her dress at a Boston party, she nearly stumbles upon an indisposed John Sullivan in a closet in the Sullivan home. After attending a performance of Augustus von Kotzebue's *The Stranger*, she narrates with mock horror an incident when her sister-in-law forgets her handkerchief: "To wipe away the tears of tragedy with a pair of gloves was indeed dreadful" (17 April).

Anna's admiration, shared by her entire family, for the novels of Jane Austen, so pronounced in the diary ("Eveg finished *Persuasion*,—& felt as if we could not bear to part with Anne Elliot & Capt Wentworth" [10 April]) continued throughout her life. An 1852 letter to her sister Susan about the family's obtaining an Austen autograph called forth an enthusiastic response: "If the house catches on fire tonight,—please save the letter—I cannot die without the sight." Eleven years later the *Atlantic Monthly* published Anna Quincy Waterston's tribute to the great British novelist.[25]

Like Austen, Anna mocks pretentious behavior. She values natural demeanor; she describes Frances Sparks as a woman with "*real* refinement, [who] is entirely free from the sickly affectation, that sometimes passes for that rare possession" (16 May). The Hill sisters impress her with their "simplicity" of dress (12 June), while in contrast Elizabeth Otis with her loud talking and extravagant apparel frequently offends her. Frederic Hoffman's innocence charms her, prompting fears that it will be "effaced by an abode in the seat of learning" (25 April). The absence of any artificiality makes Robert Storer and Henry Davis appealing, in contrast to the law student Frank Schroeder, "who left Cambridge about two years since, a delicate, modest, tho' handsome boy [but] now stood before us, a finished gentleman, fresh from the best schools of dandism that New York & Phila afford" (15 April).

Readers of Anna Quincy's 1833 diary will learn how a young woman interpreted and acted out her social role. We see her dancing at Boston cotillions and sparring with young men in the Harvard president's home. We see her weeping over Fanny Kemble's portrayal of Bianca in *Fazio* and meeting the president of the United States in Cambridge. We see her helping host a champagne celebration of her brother's engagement and dealing with the surprising appearance of Julius Tower's new wife.

In all of these activities Anna shows her keen awareness of her own privileged yet limited status in society. She dramatizes that position while also mocking society's emphasis on appearance. After viewing Fanny Kemble in *The Stranger*, she is detached enough to comment: "to have passed two evenings in weeping & *shrieking* would be deemed an odd way of being amused and really does it not seem ridiculous to go to be made to feel miserable" (17 April). Viewing dullness and pretentiousness as serious crimes, in her diary Anna aims to avoid both. She adopts the tone of an ironic observer to describe her social world. Her diary illustrates her delight in this kind of self-expression.

FURTHER READING

Austen, Jane. *Emma.*

———. *Mansfield Park.*

———. *Northanger Abbey.*

———. *Persuasion.*

———. *Pride and Prejudice.*

———. *Sense and Sensibility.*

Bunkers, Suzanne, and Cynthia Huff, eds. *Inscribing the Daily: Critical Essays on Women's Diaries.* Amherst: University of Massachusetts Press, 1996.

Cott, Nancy. *The Bonds of Womanhood.* 2d ed. New Haven: Yale University Press, 1997.

Hogan, Rebecca S. "Engendered Autobiographies: The Diary as Feminine Form." *Prose Studies* 14 (September 1991).

Kagle, Steven E. *Early Nineteenth-Century American Diary Literature.* Boston: Twayne Publishers, 1986.

Kasson, John A. *Rudeness and Civility: Manners in Nineteenth-Century Urban America.* New York: Hill and Wang, 1990.

Kerber, Linda K. *Toward an Intellectual History of Women.* Chapel Hill: University of North Carolina Press, 1997.

Lystra, Karen. *Searching the Heart: Women, Men, and Romantic Love in Nineteenth-Century America.* New York: Oxford University Press, 1990.

EDITORIAL PRINCIPLES

Transcription

1. All words in the text are transcribed as Anna Quincy (hereafter AQ) wrote them, including misspellings such as "lenght" and "usal," along with inconsistent spellings. In keeping with eighteenth- and early nineteenth-century spelling conventions, AQ used the "s" instead of the more modern "z" in such words as "Elisabeth," "sise," and "piassa," all of which have been retained. AQ's handwriting is reasonably clear; I have bracketed words that cannot be ascertained but are guesses. Occasionally, words that AQ crossed out are retained in the text in order to reflect her method of composition; changes reflecting only her simple corrections (such as "have" for "has"), however, have not been indicated. AQ's abbreviation for Cambridge ("C." or "C—") has been silently expanded after its first entry on 30 March.

2. Generally, AQ's erratic and inconsistent punctuation, with frequent use of dashes, has been retained. Commas and/or periods have sometimes been silently added to make the meaning of the sentence clearer. All superscripts have been lowered. Her occasional use of "&—" (probably intending "&c") has been converted to "&c," and her inconsistent use of single and double quotations has been regularized with double quotations. Occasionally, open or closing quotation marks have been added for clarification. Many of AQ's quoted words or phrases appear to be stylistic idiosyncrasies, since they cannot be identified.

3. For easier reading and identification, each daily entry is indicated with a new paragraph. Likewise, long entries filling several pages in the diary have been separated into paragraphs.

4. My editorial notes, italicized and in angled brackets, indicate instances where pages of the original text were cut out or words washed out. Biographical notes and other comments that AQ added later have been placed in the endnotes.

5. AQ frequently misdated entries. Her first error, dating 31 March as 30 March, has been noted in an endnote; thereafter the dates have been silently corrected.

Annotation

1. Persons appearing regularly are identified in the Biographical Directory. Others who appear only in the context of one or two entries are iden-

tified in the endnotes. Many whom AQ noted only in passing are not identified. Biographical citations are not given for persons such as Jared Sparks
or Charles Summer, who can readily be identified in the *American National Biography, Dictionary of American Biography, Quinquennial Catalogue of the Officers
and Graduates of Harvard University*, or other similar sources.

2. No note is supplied when a reference or quotation cannot be identified.

Physical description

The Anna Quincy diary, held in the Massachusetts Historical Society's
archives, is separated into three similar paperbound notebooks totaling
233 pages 8 by 6 1/2 inches, and contains entries from 14 March to 24 August 1833. AQ filled all the pages, including the back cover of volumes 1 and
3, and did not pay attention when she was nearing the end of volume 1 (see
April 30 entry). She probably wrote several entries in one sitting. For example, on 30 June she states simply, "wrote all day," and an occasional passage reads, "forgot what happened." Except for the brief diary she kept a
year later, no other has been discovered. Revealing her continued interest
in the 1833 diary are Anna's frequent brief comments added later, usually
in pencil. These often indicate the future of one of the "worthies," or comment on an event from the distance of many years. All these additions are
included as endnotes.

Previous Publication

About one-half of AQ's diary was included in Mark de Wolfe Howe's
Articulate Sisters (194–241). In order to make AQ's journal resemble a unified
narrative, Howe selected entries with a theme and gave them titles such as
"Gaieties of Boston," "A Navy Yard Excursion," and "Mount Auburn,
Grecian Art, and Trelawney." He often corrected AQ's prose as well as her
frequent misspellings. The sense of spontaneity and informality so characteristic of women's private writing is thus lost in his excerpts.

ABBREVIATIONS AND SHORT TITLES

AQ
> Anna Quincy.

CFA Diary 5 and 6
> Charles Francis Adams, *Diary of Charles Francis Adams*, ed. Marc
> Friedlaender and L. H. Butterfield, vols. 5 and 6 (Cambridge: Belknap
> Press of Harvard University Press, 1974).

Memoir
> Eliza Susan Quincy, *Memoir of the Life of Eliza S. M. Quincy* (Boston:
> John Wilson and Son, 1861).

Notes
> Anna Quincy Waterston, Autobiographical Sketch, Harvard University
> Library.

Quincy Papers
> *Papers Relating to the Quincy, Wendell, Holmes and Upham Families at the
> Massachusetts Historical Society*, ed. Marc Friedlaender and Robert Sparks
> (Boston: Massachusetts Historical Society, 1977).

Unless otherwise indicated, biographical information is drawn from standard reference works; *Quinquennial Catalogue of the Officers and Graduates of Harvard University*; unpublished records at Harvard University Archives; printed memorial class records; *Catalogue of the Officers and Students of Harvard University for the Academical Year 1832–33*; Boston city directory for 1833; and Thomas W. Baldwin, comp., *Vital Records of Cambridge* (Boston: Wright and Potter, 1914–15).

QUINCY FAMILY

Dowse, Sarah Quincy, "Aunt Dowse" (c.1757–1839), sister of Josiah Quincy Jr., married Edward Dowse 1792.

Greene, Benjamin Daniel (1793–1862), married Margaret Quincy 1826; Harvard B.A., 1812. Botanist and patron of science; lived at 50 Chesnut St., Boston.

Greene, Margaret Morton Quincy (1806–82), sister of AQ; married Benjamin Daniel Greene 1826; lived at 50 Chesnut St., Boston.

Jackson, Susan Kemper, "Aunt Jackson" (1758–1846), sister of AQ's maternal grandmother; mother of Susan Jackson Davis (see Residents of Boston and Environs).

Quincy, Abigail Phillips (1803–93), sister of AQ.

Quincy, Anna Cabot Lowell (1812–99), or AQ. Married Robert Cassie Waterston 21 April 1840 in Cambridge. Two children, Helen Ruthven (1841–1858) and Robert (1845–46).

Quincy, Edmund VII (1808–77), brother of AQ; married Lucilla Pinckney Parker 18 October 1833; Harvard M.A., 1827. Attorney, journalist, abolitionist. Law office at 27 State St., lived at 50 Chesnut St., Boston.

Quincy, Eliza Susan, "Susan" (1798–1884), sister of AQ.

Quincy, Eliza Susan Morton (1773–1850), mother of AQ; married Josiah Quincy III 1797.

Quincy, Josiah III (1772–1864), father of AQ; married Eliza Susan Morton 1797; Harvard B.A., 1790; Federalist congressman, 1805–13; mayor of Boston, 1823–28; Harvard president, 1829–45.

Quincy, Josiah IV (1802–82), brother of AQ and father of Josiah P. and Samuel M. Quincy; married Mary Jane Miller 1827; Harvard B.A., 1821. Mayor of Boston, 1846–48; railroad entrepreneur. Law office at 27 State St., lived at 4 Park St., Boston.

Quincy, Josiah Phillips (1829–1910), nephew of AQ, son of Josiah Quincy IV and Mary Jane Miller Quincy; poet, publicist.

Quincy, Maria Sophia, "Sophia" (1805–86), sister of AQ.

Quincy, Mary Jane Miller (1806–74), mother of Josiah P. and Samuel M. Quincy; married Josiah Quincy IV 1827; lived at 4 Park St., Boston.

Quincy, Samuel Miller (1832–87), nephew of AQ, son of Josiah Quincy IV and Mary Jane Miller Quincy; lawyer, Civil War officer.

Storer, Nancy, cousin of AQ; probably daughter of Hannah Quincy Storer (sister of Josiah Quincy Jr.) and Ebenezer Storer.[1]

Waterston, Robert Cassie (1812–93), son of Robert and Hepsea Lord Waterston; married AQ 21 April 1840. Unitarian minister at large, 1839–52; scholar, writer, civic leader.

QUINCY SERVANTS

WADSWORTH HOUSE, CAMBRIDGE
Betsy
Horace Bacon (Major), coachman
John
Miranda

CHESNUT ST. HOUSE, BOSTON
Bryant
Mrs. Woodward

CAMBRIDGE RESIDENTS

HARVARD STUDENTS

Chaplain, Edward K. (b. 1814), son of James (lawyer) and Eliza S. Chaplain of Cambridge, Md.; brother of William; temporary Harvard undergraduate, class of 1836.[2]

Chaplain, William Richard Thomas, "Leicester" (1811–40), son of James and Eliza S. Chaplain of Cambridge, Md.; brother of Edward; Harvard Law School student, left in 1833.[3]

Church, ———, Mr., probably Thomas Brownell Church (d. 1890) of Providence, Rhode Island; Washington College, Conn., B.A., 1831; Harvard Law School student, left in 1834.

Cleveland, Henry Russell (1808–43), brother of Horace; Harvard B.A., 1827; tutor, Harvard College.

Crafts, George Inglis (1812–92), Harvard M.A., 1837; later plantation owner outside Charleston and Confederate army officer in the Civil War.[4]

Dwight, John Sullivan (1813–93), Harvard B.A., 1832; Grad. Divinity School, 1836; later clergyman and music critic.

Gardner, Francis (1812–76), Harvard A.M., 1831; later headmaster of the Boston Latin School.

Harrison, Jesse B. (1806–41), Hampden-Sydney B.A.; Harvard LL.B., 1825; New Orleans lawyer.

Hoffman, Frederic W. (d. 1833), Harvard undergraduate, class of 1835.

Jones, Joseph Seawall (c. 1806–56), Harvard LL.B., 1833; later historian and satirist in North Carolina.[5]

May, Samuel Jr. (1810–99), Harvard M.A., 1829; Grad. Divinity School, 1833; Unitarian clergyman and abolitionist.

Minot, George (1817–58), Harvard B.A., 1836; later Boston attorney.

Minot, William (1817–94), son of William and Louisa Davis Sedgwick Minot of Boston; Harvard B.A., 1836.

Rutledge, Thomas P. (1815–38), Harvard B.A., 1835; later Charleston, S.C., merchant.

Schroeder, Charles F., Harvard Law School student, left in 1833.

Sumner, Charles (1811–74), Harvard B.A., 1830; Harvard LL.B., 1834; U.S. senator, 1851–74.

Swett, William Gray (d. 1843), Harvard A.M., 1828; Grad. Divinity School, 1831.

Vinton, Francis (1809–72), U.S. Military Academy B.S., 1830; Harvard Law School student while stationed at Fort Independence in Boston; later rector of Trinity Church, New York, 1859–69.

HARVARD FACULTY AND OTHER UNIVERSITY OFFICIALS

Alvord, James C. (1808–39), Harvard Law School professor, 1833.

Beck, Charles (1798–1866), Professor of Latin, 1832–50.

Channing, Edward Tyrell (1790–1856), brother of William Ellery; Boylston Professor of Rhetoric and Oratory, 1819–51.

Farrar, John (1779–1853), Hollis Professor of Mathematics and Natural Philosophy, 1807–36.

Felton, Cornelius (1807–62), professor of Greek, 1832–34; professor of classics, 1834–60; Harvard College president, 1860–62.

Follen, Charles C. (1796–1840), professor of German language and literature, 1830–35.

Folsom, Charles (1794–1872), Harvard librarian; editor at Harvard University Press.

Greenleaf, Simon (1783–1853), Royall Professor of Law, Harvard Law School, 1833–48.

Palfrey, John Gorham (1796–1881), dean of Harvard Divinity School, 1830–39.

Story, Joseph (1779–1845), Dane Professor of Law, 1829–45; U.S. Supreme Court justice, 1811–45; member of Harvard Corporation in 1833.

Ware, Henry Jr. (1794–1843), professor of Pulpit Eloquence and the Pastoral Care, 1840–42.

Ware, Henry Sr. (1764–1845), Hollis Professor of Divinity, 1805–40.

OTHER CAMBRIDGE RESIDENTS AND VISITORS

Channing, Henrietta Ellery, Mrs. Edward T.

Craigie, Elizabeth Shaw, Mrs. Andrew (1772–1842).

Farrar, Elizabeth Rotch (1791–1870), author of The Young Lady's Friend and The Children's Robinson Crusoe; married John Farrar 1828.

Higginson, Susan Channing, married Dr. Francis T. Higginson 1831.

Hill, Hannah (d. 1837), daughter of Harriet Quincy and Aaron Hill; married Willard Phillips 1833.

Hill, Harriet Quincy, Mrs. Aaron (1762–1839), cousin of AQ.[6]

Hoffman, Ann, of Baltimore, Md., sister of Frederic.

Robinson, Therese Albertina von Jakob (1797–1869), married Edward Robinson, professor at Andover Theological Seminary, 1828. German native; translator and scholar; author of The Slavic Languages and Literature, among other publications.

Sparks, Frances Anne Allen (d. 1835), married Jared Sparks 1832.

Sparks, Jared (1789–1866), married Frances Allen 1832; editor, North American Review until 1830; edited the Papers of George Washington 1833–37; president of Harvard University, 1849–53.

Story, Sarah Waldo Wetmore (1784–1855), married Joseph Story 1808.

Wells, William (1773–1860), Harvard B.A., 1796; classical scholar; head of school for young men in Cambridge from 1830.[7]

Biographical Directory

Adams, Abigail Brooks (1808–89), married Charles Francis Adams 1829; lived at 3 Hancock St.

Adams, Charles Francis (1807–86), son of president John Quincy Adams, cousin of AQ; Boston lawyer; U.S. minister to Great Britain, 1861–68, lived at 3 Hancock St.

Bromfield, John, probably John D. Bromfield (1779–1849), Boston merchant and philanthropist.[8]

Cleveland, Horace W. G. (1814–1900), brother of Henry; former secretary to his father in Havana; Boston clerk; later landscape architect.

Codman, John (1808–79), Boston lawyer.[9]

Davis, Henry (Charles Henry) (1807–77), brother of Louisa Davis Minot; Harvard student who became a midshipman traveling to the Pacific and the Mediterranean before returning to Cambridge. Harvard B.A., 1841; later rear admiral in the Civil War and superintendent of the Naval Observatory.

Davis, Isaac P. (1771–1855), husband of Susan Jackson Davis, father of Thomas K. and George Davis. Boston merchant and manufacturer; lived at 8 Winthrop Place.[10]

Davis, Susan Jackson (c. 1785–1867), cousin of AQ, mother of Thomas K. and George Davis; married Isaac P. Davis 1807; lived at 8 Winthrop Place.[11]

Davis, Thomas K. (1808–53), son of Isaac P. and Susan Jackson Davis; Harvard B.A., 1827; Boston lawyer.

Dwight, Thomas (d. 1876), Harvard B.A., 1827; Boston lawyer; lived at 52 Chesnut St.[12]

Forbes, Robert Bennet (1804–89), Boston shipping merchant; lived in Milton.

Gore, John C. (c. 1806–60), son of Boston merchant John Gore (d. c. 1817) and Mary Babcock Gore Russell; painter who studied in Florence from 1829 to 1832.[13]

Gore, Louisa Ingersoll (1813–91), daughter of Boston merchant John Gore (d. c. 1817), and Mary Babcock Gore Russell; married sculptor Horatio Greenough 1837;[14] lived in Jamaica Plain.

Grant, Anna Powell Mason (c. 1789–1861), mother of Elizabeth Grant; lived at 55 Mt. Vernon St.[15]

Grant, Elizabeth (1811–69), daughter of Patrick and Anna Powell Mason Grant; lived at 55 Mt. Vernon St.[16]

Gray, Francis C. (1790–1856), Harvard M.A., 1809; Massachusetts legislator; member of Harvard Corporation, 1826–36, lived at 57 Summer St.

Guild, Eliza Eliot (b. c. 1790), mother of Eliza Quincy Gould; married Boston attorney Benjamin Guild 1817; lived in Brookline.

Guild, Eliza Quincy, daughter of Eliza and Benjamin Guild; lived in Brookline.

Miller, Samuel Ridgway, father of Mary Jane Miller Quincy; Boston merchant; lived at 4 Park St.

Miller, Mrs. Samuel Ridgway, wife of Samuel Ridgway Miller, mother of Mary Jane Miller Quincy; lived at 4 Park St.

Minot, Louisa Davis Sedgwick (d. 1858), mother of Mary and William Minot, sister of Charles Henry Davis; married William Minot 1809;[17] lived at 58 Beacon St.

Minot, Mary (Maria) (1811–82), daughter of William and Louisa Davis Sedgwick Minot;[18] lived at 58 Beacon St.

Minot, William Sr. (1783–1873), husband of Louisa Davis Sedgwick Minot, father of Mary and William Minot. Harvard M.A., 1802; Boston lawyer; lived at 58 Beacon St.

Otis, Eliza Boardman (1796–1873), widow of Harrison Gray Otis Jr., lived at 8 Somerset St.

Parker, Daniel Pinckney (1781–1850), husband of Mary Weeks Parker, father of Lucilla and Henry Tuke Parker; Boston merchant;[19] lived at 40 Beacon St.

Parker, Henry Tuke (1824–90), son of Daniel P. and Mary Weeks Parker; Harvard B.A., 1842; lived at 40 Beacon St.

Parker, Lucilla (1810–60), daughter of Daniel P. and Mary Weeks Parker; married Edmund Quincy 18 October 1833; lived at 40 Beacon St.

Parker, Mary Weeks (d. 1863), mother of Lucilla and Henry Parker; married Daniel Parker 1806;[20] lived at 40 Beacon St.

Phillips, Abigail (1814–69), married Edward Salisbury 1836.[21]

Pickering, John (1777–1846), Harvard B.A., 1796; Boston lawyer; Harvard Overseer; lived at 74 Beacon St.

Russell, Dutton (born James Russell Dutton) (1810–61), Harvard B.A., 1829; Boston lawyer.[22]

Russell, Mary Babcock Gore (d. 1836), mother of Louisa and John C. Gore, wife of Boston merchant Joseph Russell;[23] lived in Jamaica Plain.

Salisbury, Abigail Breeze (1780–1866), widow of Josiah Salisbury; lived on Mt. Vernon St.[24]

Salisbury, Edward (1814–1901), son of Josiah and Abigail Salisbury; Yale B.A., 1832; later professor of Asian languages at Yale; married Abigail Phillips 1836; lived on Mt. Vernon St.

Salisbury, Martha (1812–52), daughter of Josiah and Abigail Breeze Salisbury; married Theodore Dwight Woolsey 1833; lived on Mt. Vernon St.

Sargent, Howard (d. 1872), Harvard B.A., 1829, Harvard M.D., 1832.

Sargent, John Osborne (1811–91), Harvard B.A., 1830; studied law in Boston; later Harvard Overseer.

Storer, Robert B. (1796–1870), married Sarah Sherman Hoar c. 1835 and had five children from 1838 to 1845. Merchant; later engaged in Russian trade; lived on Hancock St.[25]

Welles, John (d. 1855), Harvard M.A., 1782; merchant; Harvard Overseer; lived at 59 Summer St.

❧ The Diary ❧

Friday 17 – dull day – drew – commenced
my first drawing in water colours – note
it down, so that if I ever become
a great Artist, this leaf — may be placed
in some great collection of valuable
records! — To you, my dear Mrs Greene
I dedicate it, as it was with the
colours presented by you, this great
genius, first flourished a brush. –
Mr Hoffman called – as pleasing as ever
Saturday 18th. Went into town while
Mama went on to Dedham. Called
at Lucilla's. I had a two hours gossip
with her – heard descriptions of Miss
Kemble's last appearance &c – and also
of the pamphlet entitled 'Scenes at
the fair' – imputed to Mrs Barillo – very
well done, but very impertinent. –
Dined with Lucilla, I passed the P. le
with Matthew – Returned to C. Mr
Fallowe in the evng –
Sunday 19th. Did not go to church in the
morng – Mr Wall dined here. –

Diary entries for 17–19 May 1833

CHAPTER 1

The Harvard University Community

March 1833

Anna Quincy wrote most of her journal entries at the president's house in Cambridge. Until her marriage in 1840, she lived in Wadsworth House, a place she referred to as "our cottage." Hardly a cottage, but rather a spacious dwelling, the 1726 building where the Quincys lived still stands on Massachusetts Avenue, today housing alumni offices. Harvard University and Cambridge, however, have greatly changed from the days when carriages rolled down the street and an open market selling country produce occupied the space that has become Harvard Square.[1]

Anna's father, Josiah Quincy, assumed the Harvard presidency in 1829 and served in that capacity until 1845. He and Anna's mother, Eliza Morton Quincy, set the social tone in the little village of Cambridge. As the daughter of the university's president, Anna, along with the rest of her family, had the responsibility of entertaining Harvard students and faculty members. Rarely a day passed that Anna did not note visits from some member of the Harvard community.

In 1833 Harvard University was a small aspiring institution, while Cambridge, a town of slightly more than six thousand residents, was surrounded by farms. Only 212 students—all men—were enrolled as undergraduates, with 166 graduate students in the law, divinity, and medical schools. Professors and instructors for all of these totaled just 23 men, all living nearby, many on Professors Row (later Kirkland Street). Only a handful of classrooms and dormitories made up Harvard University, although some students lodged in rooming houses nearby. All dined in the commons at University Hall, which also housed the chapel. The formation of what is now the famed Harvard "Yard" began during Josiah Quincy's presidency.[2]

The undergraduates whom Anna describes (for example, Thomas Rutledge) had already passed entrance examinations in Latin and Greek (including Cicero's *Orations* and the four gospels of the New Testament), mathematics, and geography. In the first two years of their curriculum these students concentrated on the classics and mathematics; in their last two years the young men pursued more wide-ranging subjects, including philosophy, political economy, physics, and chemistry.[3]

Most of Anna's caustic comments are directed toward graduate students in their early to mid-twenties who were studying in the law and divinity schools. Divinity students such as John Sullivan Dwight and Samuel May had to demonstrate knowledge of Hebrew, Greek, and Latin; in their three years at Harvard they studied theology, ecclesiastical history, and ministerial duties. The law school required no entrance examination, but applicants were obliged to supply a statement of previous studies. If an applicant was a Harvard graduate, as was Charles Sumner, he could obtain a degree in three years; others, such as William Chaplain and Joseph Seawall Jones, must study for five years. Law students pursued standard subjects grounded in the English common law and in Equity: contracts, property law, constitutional and public law. Harvard stipulated that all applicants to any class or school "must exhibit proper testimonials of a good moral character." Tuition and room charges for the separate schools ranged from $66 to $100; board was $1.75 a week. Wood could be delivered for about $7 a cord (unsplit wood was a dollar cheaper).[4]

As president, Josiah Quincy exercised his responsibilities in an office annexed to the Wadsworth House, on the second floor. Harvard was governed in those days by the Corporation, a group of seven men who administered the university's financial and personnel matters, and the Board of Overseers, a larger group meeting less frequently to develop broader policies. The Corporation set the salaries for administration and faculty; in 1833 Quincy received $2,235, while professors such as Henry Ware Sr. and Edward T. Channing were paid $1500, and Cornelius Felton $1,000.[5]

Except for the minor fracas that Anna reports on 30 May, no student eruptions occurred during the 1832–33 academic term while she kept her journal. Loyal to "Papa," Josiah's youngest daughter would no doubt have dismissed the criticism he incurred from some quarters for his heavy-handed governing. On the other hand, some graduates, such as Charles Eliot Norton, later recalled that President Quincy enjoyed "excellent" relations with the Harvard students: "much like that of a colonel to the men of his regiment who feel that, though he commands them, he is still one with them in interest and in sympathy." Indeed, Quincy became renowned for his energetic, hands-on, and businesslike leadership.[6]

During his presidency, Quincy sought to impose stiffer admission requirements and a classical curriculum at Harvard. He also tried to add a tone of civility to the campus. Andrew Peabody, who was a tutor in 1833, later recalled how the president "relieve[d] the rudeness of the barrack life to which [undergraduate] students were then subjected by the isolation of the college, and by the rules which forbade absence from town [Boston] except on Saturday." These students thus welcomed the hospitality that the Quincys offered at Wadsworth House. On Thursdays while the college was in session (first weekly and later every other week), Josiah and Eliza Morton Quincy, along with their "amiable and accomplished family," received visitors in their home. According to Anna, Wadsworth House's "long low rooms" were "furnished & arranged with simple, but elegant taste [and] well fitted for 'living rooms' and reception rooms." Of these soirées one student boasted that "some of the best representatives of Boston society were usually present. The President moved round among his guests, a living embodiment of stately and elegant manners."[7]

In 1886, as Anna Waterston, Anna lamented that more recent Harvard students in the late nineteenth century "little dream of the hosts of fair women and brave men, the learned, the eloquent, the distinguished, who have passed through its apartments."[8] But if the seventy-four-year-old Anna had consulted her 1833 diary, she would have found there few descriptions of brave or distinguished men among the many visitors to Wadsworth House.

March 1833

Thursday March 14th 1833— The last image of you, my dear Margy, which is left upon my imagination, was the "broad disk" of yr prodigious black cloak, as you scrambled into that vast & uncertain region called the inside of a stage coach,[9] & even that vision was soon shrouded from my aching sight, & the last wheel of yr equipage as it departed rolled methought merrily away, one good omen at least for your journey— Like the uncertainty of what is before you, does the vacant pages of my journal book glare, in my face, and as little do those who go, or those who stay, know what is to come—but as I do not mean to sentimentalise I will leave the future to the fates, and in recording each passing hour, whether sad or gay leave at least some remembrance of what has occurred during the time you are far awa'.— After your departure we "packed up our tatters", not thank fortune, to follow a *drum*, but to be driven by a Major, & soon after, bidding adieu for the *last* time *to Chesnut Street*, drove to Miss [Lalarmes], &

secured the miniature, which I think very good; then went to Mrs Russell & Mama to Mrs Millers— Passed half an hour which Louisa in talking over the last evening &c &c Then walked up to Chesnut St, where we met the carriage & taking bundles without control, fled back to the classic shades—wisely contented with our humble bower, which we had not been tempted to leave, by the "dream of Ambition of honor or power"— no, tho' they came in the Shape of a Musidora,[10] or Quimby—or a gold mine! After dinner wearied by conflicting emotions I sunk to my slumbers, & have but this moment awoke to tell my story—& having nothing more to say bid you adieu for today—a Rhyme, almost equal to—"Mr May are you blown away"—"or Mrs Ware take a chair."

Friday 15th The snow storm this morning quite distressed us, as we feared it might be the cause of detaining your party in Providence but the Sun has now come out, & I suppose you are even now dashing away to N Y. The visitors this morning were Sir John Caldwell— Sir John, is a very pleasing man of about 40—animated & agreeable— Mr Sargent toujours le même—entertained me with an account of some adventures in N. Y. which were really gratifying. In the evening read loud in the German Prince.[11] Mr Perry came in, & passed an hour quite agreeably— I thought he was safe at Newport, as I took a touching farewell of his "glorious black eyes," about three months ago—& they have been beaming upon Divinity Hall ever since.—

Saturday 16th Went into Town with Mama, who was on her muddy way to Dedham. Went to see Martha—& Lucilla then to Louisas—went with her to call on The Audubons & the eagle—found—Mr Channing the minister there also, & really the eyes of Mr Channing Mr Audubon, & the Eagle together were worth seeing.[12]— Dined at Mrs Russells—drank tea at Mrs Millers, & then came out of town.

Sunday 17— Morng did not go to church— Mr Wells & Elisa Guild dined here— Elisa seemed in very good spirits, & we laughed right merrily-— The Chaplain nonsense going on in the same style the Walker topic used to be discussed—Afternoon—Mr Palfrey—Josiah, Edmund & Horace Cleveland our only visitors.

Monday 18th Drew &c— Afternoon Mrs Stearns came Evening, Papa, Susan & I drove to the City about ½ past 8. to a party at Mrs A Lawrences[13]-— We had a pleasant drive in, although we nearly broke our necks, & the horses legs in endeavouring to reach the door of our elevated host,— At last however we were safely lodged in the take off room, &

Etching of Wadsworth House by Susan Quincy, c. 1840. ". . . walked up to Chesnut St, where we met the carriage & taking bundles without control, fled back to the classic shades—wisely contented with our humble bower" (14 March 1833). Originally built in 1727 for Harvard University president Benjamin Wadsworth, the house served as a presidential residence until 1849. At one time the centerpiece of extensive grounds, today it faces busy Massachusetts Avenue and is occupied by Harvard's alumni offices. Courtesy of Harvard University Archives, Cambridge, Mass.

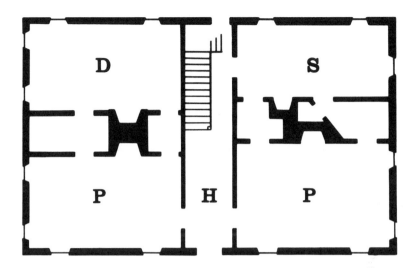

Floor plan of Wadsworth House, Cambridge. The entrance to the house is at the bottom of this drawing. Initials (P for parlor, H for hall, D for dining room, and S for study) indicating the main downstairs rooms are conjectures only. The large darkened areas separating the rooms indicate fireplaces. A kitchen ell is not included in this floor plan. Drawing by Susan Maycock, courtesy of the Cambridge Historical Commission, Cambridge, Mass.

after adonising a little, descended—& were met by mine host & hostess, with open arms— But a small part of the company had assembled & our own family seemed to compose the greater part of it—

There were about hundred persons in all, of every shape sise & dimension, & from the variety of modes which the eccentric lady had used in her invitations some came in ball dresses, flowers & feathers, while some were in simple home attire— But the various *persons*, were nothing to the variety of things which were cram'd into these devoted apartments— I never saw any thing to equall it.— Pictures of every shape, sise, & hue, were hung, or rather pitched upon the walls, with but the slightest regard to conformity— Book Shelves filled with books, & boxes & shells, & stuffed birds, & china pitchers, & plants, & flowers & Sugar ornaments, & bronses, & hook & eye boxes full of seals, & states & china manderines & paper baskets, & gold snuff boxes, & birds nests, & butterflies, were all mingled higgety piggly as I have enumerated them, & I do not believe that any one would credit the catalogue of this museum, who has not been an eye witness— I never beheld any thing like it, & it really seemed as if Mrs L. must have gone up into all the garrets of the museums, & neighbouring houses, & showered down, upon her hapless mansion all the old odd things, that ever were stored away.—

One room becoming crowded I went into the other with Henry Davis who seemed very dull, but could not help laughing as at every turn we met some oddity, or other. He at last lodged me under the spreading branches of a myrtle tree, the birds to be sure were not singing in its branches, but a defunct birds nest was suspended from one of them, which answered the same purpose.— Here I was joined by my *favorite* Mr. John Audubon,—whose remarks I will pass over—next bowed—up Mr Armstrong, walking on his head a little higher than usual, with all the expresment of a Lt Govr. & all the sweetness & delightfulness possible— we had quite a small firtation until my lord, seeing the Gov enter—bows low, & vanishes, saying "I must go & pay my respects to my Commander in Chief" "Tis aromatic vinegar indeed!!"[14]

Being now left alone in my glory, I espied Mr Frothingham, ~~not~~ disengaged a few paces from me,—making a bold stroke—for a clergyman. I wreathed a remarkable smile & in order to pussle the worthy man, as I knew he did not know me from Adam—says I, "good eveg. Mr Frothingham, how do you do"— Mr Frothingham, gathered up his wits, & with a bewildered air, bows in return, making the same enquiry, as much as to say—"who the—wonder are you"— "Ah Mr Frothingham," say I, "I fancy you do not remember me, so to set you right at once, I am Miss Quincy"— "Oh Miss Quincy, I am delighted to see you. I thought it was the face of a *Capulet*"[15] (Is the man mad thought I, looking in my turn rather bewildered.)— "I've just been telling yr sister," says he, "that the Capulets are pretty strong tonight. I never knew you before I believe, but if yr name is Quincy, I must admire you as I do every thing of that name."— I thanked him for my share & we continued to chirp on in this manner for some time—

At last through the folding doors appears Mrs Inglis' with a thing upon her head which can only be compared to the Egyptian paintings on Sarcophagus' & being placed directly over her eyebrows, she would have passed very well for the reanimated form of some *fair Egyptian* who had been "shut up in a chest" some few centuries. I never saw its like before or behind either, & I should have advised Mrs. Lawrence to have procured it when the eveg was over to *Cap* the Climax of her cabinet of curiosities—

As this vision of beauty met our astonished gase, Mr Frothingham & myself at the same moment glared first at her, & then at each other & unable to command our risibles fell into a most unclerical & unCapulet fit of laughter.

But we were soon arrested by the sounds which most musical, most melancholy, floated through the door way, & which sounded like the dirge of some of the defunct birds, or beasts, or perchance Egyptians, whose corporeal frames surrounded the apartment— It proved however to be "Erin, the tear & the smile", which was wailed forth by Miss Bond & Miss May, & certainly the *tear* [secured] "to [hear] the belle & have the majority," in their opinion, as a more doleful strain never greeted my ears. It had quite the effect of an antedote to Mrs Inglis' turban, & even Mr Frothingham who has been known to sing "come rest in this bosom", remarked that a more lively air would be desirable at a party[16]—Just at this moment he seises my hand & gallants me up to Mrs Frothingham, & introduces me, we just "scraped back our foot, bobbed our heads at each other & away", as old Mr Reynolds says, for she was conversing with some manly form, & at the same moment the handsome Brewster, in a magnificent scarlet waistcoat, addressed me, so Mr Frothingham vanished— Mr Brewster was handsome & gentlemanly but is not particularly interesting.

Just then I beheld a long table being laid in the same apartment with a white table cloth, a waiter[17] placed at the head, garnished with cups & saucers, looking for all the world like a breakfast table— "Pray" said I to Mr Brewster, "am I utterly uncivilised, or is not this some thing new—to breakfast at midnight"— Mr B. turned his fine eyes for a moment in the direction of the table, & remarked that he believed he had seen the same fashion the other evening at Mrs Otis' but that really any thing new was refreshing now, "every thing was so common".— I of course agreed, tho' certainly making a mental reservation in favor of Mrs L's party, which certainly had the merit of being uncommon.— In order to enliven my wearied swain, I proposed a walk into the next apartment in search of something if not *new* at least strange— Accordingly we wandered away.—

In the centre of the apartment stood Mr Bates, who giving me a glance intended to go directly to my heart, assured me of the felicity it gave him to behold me once more. Probably the happiness was too much for his sensibilities, for the instant after he turned his back & vanished. Mr Hooper then came up; & I released Mr Brewsters arm, & talked to him some time— Mrs Lawrence then waved us into the other room, to the Supper table— The Chocolate, for which the cups & saucers appeared, sent up a fragrant steam from the nose of a matronly coffee pot, & seemed to be the Chaperone of the rest of the viands— By way of light & airy nothings there was a candied pyramid of oranges & all other little affairs that constitute a supper— The crowd was immense, & the babel of tongues passes all understanding—in every sense of the word.— Howard Sargent then came up, & Mr Dixwell, & we had—much laugh about nothing, & many witty things said which are not worth recording. As soon as possible, I took Mr Sargents arm, & went into the other room, & soon after Papa came up & said the carriage was waiting— Mrs L waved & curtsied, & thanked all the Capulets for coming, including Howard Sargent in the general sweep—but I suppose he might pass for county "Paris", for to do him justice he is rather too good—or too handsome for the Apothecary.— In the take off—or rather the put on room, we found Mrs [J] Gardner & Tom Davis. Mrs G. was in a great frolic having found a large *pistol* on the mantlepiece— I thought this was the finishing stroke, & had some idea of firing a parting salute, in order like Mrs Rafferty to have a taste of every thing at this Tusculum.[18] At the door, while we were waiting till the carriage could be found, which on a dark night in Somerset St. is no easy matter, Mr Frothingham, gaily trips up to me, "Just in time to say farewell to you" said he, with infinite promptitude. "Do not hurry yrself, Mr Frothingham," says I, "for theres no prospect of our going this half hour"— However the parting hour was nearer than I anticipated, & having said like Mr Vinton, "Farewell", I gave "my hand—to Lord Howard, & sprang" into the carriage— A more diverting evening, I have seldom passed, & merrily did I laugh over it—had a pleasant drive home, which we reached about [½] past 11 o'ck.—

Tuesday 19th A letter from you, my dear Margy, was right welcome unto us, this morning, as it announced yr safe arrival in N.Y.— Mama & Sophia went to town— Susan & I drew—& I wrote a letter to you. About 12 a gig drives to the door, Mr & Mrs Whitwell are announced, as wishing to see me. Of course, we desended & found my friend Mr Whitwell & his wife, who had come out to see me, before going to Europe.— The idea of their taking the trouble to come out to see a damsel of my standing was really amusing, however it seemed really to be from the kindness of their feelings— Mr Whitwell & I struck up a great friendship, when we met at Norfolk, & he really seemed to be quite interested in our acquaintance—

They are truly excellent persons, & Mr W very agreeable & gentlemanly—
they paid us a long visit & then took a most affectionate farewell. Hoping
to renew our friendship on their return, which I am sure I shall be most
happy to do.— The rest of the day passed without visitors.

Wednesday 20th Stormy day, which was rather unpropitious for the
Miller fête to which we were engaged—this evening. We, however hoped
it would clear before night— Vain hope, for "as the night drew drearer,"
we were rather nonplused to know what to do. Dire was the debating &
varied the expedients, but how to go in & come out through rain, mud, &
darkness was not to be determined, at last we decided that Mama Susan &
I should go in, & stay all night at Chesnut Street—& therefore literally
packing up our clothes in a bandbox, (tho' no Dashwood was at hand to
receive—or rather to deceive us,)[19] we bade adieu to Sophia, who was left
alone in her glory, & "flew by night" to Chesnut St.— The silvertoned
Woodward saluted our entrance, & was some what taken *aback* I believe,
by this irruption. However our graceful manners soon won her heart, &
proceeding onwards to the parlour, I spied a few sparks in the grate
which were soon enkindled into a flame— Mama determined to dress in
the parlour, while Susan & I repaired to the tobacco plantation upstairs—
& I hope the perfume did not accompany us to the party, for tho' it may be
forgiven as the atmosphere surrounding *manly* beauty, it would scarcely
be advantageous to the fair sex.— While we were all in the parlour Edmund came in, & was rather bewildered, but all sweetness—

At ½ past 8 o'clk we drove to Mrs Millers— Found one or two ladies in
the take off room. Soon desended & were met by Mrs Miller & Mary Jane,
with much cordiality — The people came very late—about fifty in all—
Talked first to Mr Sprague, who quite captivated me—then to Elisabeth
Grant, who looked very pretty,—then to Charles Adams,—Mr Vinton Mr
Jones—John Codman &c&c— About ½ past nine, the doors opened, & a
very handsome supper table appeared,— Mr Fessenden armed me in, but
that was all I saw of the stout gentleman, for after he had supplied me
with a plate of blancmange, with which by the way he gave me no spoon,
(expecting I suppose I should eat à la Eve,) he vanished or at least, his
place being taken by Mr Chaplain, I doubt whether *his* image ever crossed
my mind—again— Mr Chaplain, was more *present* than usual, & in our
half hours talk, seemed quite like himself— We should have had a very
agreeable supper, had not Mr Jones, immediately taken his stand behind
us, & putting in his oar continually quite spoiled our "soul breathing in-

tercourse." However Mr J. will not long trouble us in any way, as he tells me, he *rows* off on Monday—"unwept, unhonored, & unsung"—[20]

I wish the departures stopt there, and we should be quite contented—but alas—Mr Chaplain told me that his residence in Cambridge, was also drawing to a close, & although he had fully intended staying two years, circumstances had occurred at home, which must recall him— "To meet & part is mortals lot"—& we ought by this time to be used to it— Though we "are steel" as Elisa Guild says, we are not quite hard enough yet—iron perhaps is the best material—but I am growing sentimental & if I go on with steel & iron, I shall come soon, to *flints*, which we all know are akin to sparks, & then comes tinder, & *flames*, & we may be all in a blase before I get to the end—of my page, so I hasten back to the party—

where was I— oh we were at the supper table, an excellent place to dispel sentiment— I do not remember any thing that was said worthy to be immortalised in my journal, tho' much of it did very well—at the time & some of it is remembered,— The ladies all returning to the other room, Mr Jones stuck out his elbow, which much against my will I took, & we returned also.— Robert Hooper then came up, but did not captivate me, for tho' very handsome he has no refinement— A catillon was called,— which I danced with Mr Jones which was rendered more agreeable in having, Mr Vinton as a vis à vis, & Mr Chaplain, at my *corner*.— After this cotillion the company in general departed— We that is to say our party—Edmund, Lucilla & Tom Davis, then took our seat at the Supper table, & had quite a pleasant time— Altogether the party went off very well & I think was quite an animated one.—

When we went up stairs, we went into the nursery, where the two children were asleep, & truly it was the prettiest sight; we saw that evening—These two beautiful children, so quietly & sweetly sleeping, looked like some lovely picture & indeed seemed but little lower than the cherubs. We could not but contrast this pretty very pretty picture with the scene we had just left—& could hardly believe that the men & women, who had been dressing, & flirting & eating & drinking, could once have been such little darlings—[21] We remained upstairs some time, while Mary Jane & Mrs Miller joined us, and [??ome] We talked over the evening—in all its particulars and all agreed it had gone off very well— We then took leave & departed— Passed the night in yr apartment but did not see your blithesome ghost.

Thursday 21st Came out of town—talked over the eveg &c— The day was lowring, chilly, dark, the roads were deep & boggy, the night was dark & foggy, & we of course did not anticipate any of "our hens" would *peck* their way out here— Indeed we should have been sorry to have seen any one from Boston— We had all the Cambridge worthies & all our elite beaux, & only regretted we had not more belles— Mr Rutlegdge first approached me, putting to flight some inferior being, who was daring to address me, we were soon joined by Mr Jones, who certainly would be classed by Mr [Gasport?] under the "*Voluables;*" these two youths amused *themselves* some time, & entertained me until the superior form of Mr Chaplain approached & then they spread their wings, biddy gutterfies, as they are, & left the scene to Chaplain—& to me As the elevated & the refined, however they surpass the ~~frivolous &~~ ridiculous & the unmeaning, in actual merit, & agreeableness, is not as well fitted to entertain in the pages of a journal, I more frequently record the sayings of a Jones & a Vinton, rather than a Chaplains, tho' far more worthy.

I therefore pass over the next half hour, during which we took a tour into the next apartment, wandered for some time gasing at the varied beauties of Nature & art & at lenght paused to moralise before the declaration of independance,—which if "you recollect yourself my good girl", hangs over the fire place, in which was enkindled a hospitable flame,— But we were *above* such considerations & *stept* over the *fender*, in order to view more nearly same ancient worthy— While we were standing the *fire* of *patriotism,* Sophia & Mr Vinton approached,—& Mr Vinton with infinite humour, jocosely addressed us on the subject of our insensibility to all things around us, even to the elements.— The haughty Leicester is the last person I should select to *rally* jocosely on any subject, & suddenly withdrawing from the offending fender, without taking any notice of Mr Vintons remarks, offered his arm, & "we sailed away to more secure repose"—& took our station before the shrine of *Lafayette*—[22]

Here we enjoyed the flow of soul for some time, & were deeply engaged in some interesting ~~disquis~~ topic, when without the least preparation, Mr Vintons *head* was thrust directly before us, in so startling a manner that even Leicester—started, & I almost leapt into the air— Barbarous man! He broke the illusion, merely to ask me who that young lady was—meaning Miss Randall. He then proceeded to remark that my sister was "so kind, & very obliging that she had gone upstairs to bring done a small glass bird for him"— Thinks I the man is demented entirely, what on Earth can he mean—

"Glass bird" repeated I, with a bewildered air, reflected *faintly* indeed, from the glance of my elevated companion. "Yes", resumed Mr Vinton, "I believe it is a Peacock, at any rate it has a *long tail* of spun glass". This explanation, though it threw light upon me, seemed to cap the climax of Leicesters amasement. With folded arms, & knit brows, he looked down upon us, with a glance that might have melted the spun glass of the Peacocks tail. I hastened to explain the glassworkers powers & then turned the conversation—while Mr Vinton skipt off.— Soon after Miss Randall was prevailed upon to play—which she did extremely well. Soon after Sophia & Mr Vinton armed with the glass birds—approached— Sophia declared that when she showed the wonderful bird with the glass tail to Leicester that he like Mr Meadows took no sort of notice of it—while Mr Vintons more present soul, exclaimed, "wonderful beautiful, exquiste"— and such is the praise of which *she* is silly enough to be vain— Miss Randall again played—and is certainly a first rate performer I should think, tho' I must confess, mere instrumental music gives me but very little pleasure except when I am all alone.—

Talked to Rutledge some time—silly child—and then again to Mr Vinton, who is certainly an [amusing] personage.— He informed me that he was certain we had "one comfort in our house"— "A great many—Mr Vinton, but to which do you allude" "Why" said he "I just looked in to the little parlour, & there I saw a woman, most industriously *plying her needle*, quite regardless of the company— I am sure she must be a treasure"!— *Betsy* certainly little imagined, that she was the object of Mr Vintons attention—but I agreed & then followed an account of some *old family servants'* of the *noble race of Vinton!* I then thought I would go a touch beyond—, so I told him that we had a still more distinguished member, and entered into a description of our coachman, who was a Major of artillery!— <*one page appears to be cut off here*> His astonishment was great, (second only to the Peacock with a glass tail)— "Is it possible" exclaimed he. "A major of Artillery! why, Miss Quincy if we were called in to service, that man would rank above me"! Just at this moment the Major appeared, bearing in his hand not a sword, but a waiter, which he offered to us— As soon as he had passed & turned away—Mr Vinton raises his hand to make the military salute, & bowing low says "I pay my respects to my Superior officer"— It was quite smart of the youth I thought & certainly done very well.—

We then returned to the other room, where we had again a long & sentimental conversation, during which he enquired if I could inform him, how a gentleman was to know ~~how far~~ if he had penetrated into a ladys heart far enough to offer his own! I replied "really Mr V I must leave that to yr own penetration". "Oh" said he "I was not referring to myself— I am now in a mere *butterfly* State, *roving* from flower to flower but it was more for the future I wished to be informed"— Leaving Mr Vinton in his butterfly state, I lightly flew off & had varied talks with various mortals, & wound up the evening with a talk with Mr Jones of which no trace is left on my memory— We had a pleasant evening & so ended the Levées of 1833.—

Friday 22d— Fine day— drew all the morning, in the afternoon had a letter from Abby & yrslf at Phila. In the evening Sophia & I drove in to town, to attend a party at the John Welles'. Dressed at Chesnut St found to my no small discomforture that I had not brought in the belt to my dress—despatched Bryant to Louisa Gores, to ask her for hers, as I knew she had a dress like mine. Sent me one that did very well but said she had on the *dress* & of course the belt— About 9 went to Mrs Welles'— Saw, as we entered, some personages that looked marvellously like *musicians*, thought it was going to be a supper party, & therefore wore an old pair of *shoes*, but 'twas vain to weep—& therefore ascended— Were quite early. Received in the drawing room, the folding doors closed Talked to the Welles' who were all as polite as possible— Heard the new engagement for the first time—The Nabob, to Miss L. Gardiner "Gracious me," what sayings & what doings there will be— Then talked to Tom Amory &c &c Company fast assembling—

About ½ past 9 the folding doors flew open as if by majic, & the music burst forth— The effect was very fine, & we quickly trod the floor. My attendant was the light & airy Mr Nat Bowditch, not an Apollo to be sure but very well to begin with— Mr Wolcott next requested my hand but I was engaged to Mr Geo: Bethune! with whom I performed the next cotillon, then came young Mr Salisbury (*not* the heir apparent)[23] with whom I *hammered* thro' a dance— Mr T. Dwight actually exerted himself to come across the room to engage my hand for the next, a stretch of politeness quite overwhelming— During this dance Mr Vinton approached & smiled so sweetly in my e'e, that I turned from Mr Salisbury. Mr Vinton requested the next dance— Cruel fate! I was engaged—we then entered into a light & *airy butterfly* conversation, & among other things, I told Mr V. how I had been deceived into wearing an old pair of shoes to the party. "An old pair of shoes" exclaimed he, "I *doat upon old shoes*, they are the most *delightful* things in the world"— Complaisant creature—who can even doat upon old shoes!—[24]

Mr Jones now joined us, & requested also the happiness of the next dance, but that felicity had been forestalled. When the dance concluded, the door into the little parlour was opened, & there in was seen a very pretty Supper. Mr Dwight proposed going in, & we accordingly entered. Found a cool & agreeable place in a window, & various nice things. Mr Bassett also joined us, & we had a very pleasant time we staid there during two cotillons, & it was by far the pleasantest part of the eveg— When we reached the dancing room the third cotillon was commencing So we went into the drawing room & lit upon two delightful blue damask arm chairs & there we sat until that dance ended conversing very agreeably— Hearing the last link of the cotillon broken, we started off to take our places, but our dance seemed to recede as we advanced, & this time was changed to a waltz— This of course we did not join, but remained spectators of the *exhibition* which it pleased Mrs Otis & Miss Marshall Mr Parish & John Sullivan to give us—[25] I really felt tempted to exclaim with Mr Elliot "arn't you ashamed!", & never felt more disagreeably—standing between Mr Dwight, & Mr Jones, & witnessing such a display. At lenght it ended & we were at last enabled to perform the dance.— The next danced with John Codman, who was, as he ever is extremely agreeable, & on this evening very animated— Next with John O Sargent, & then it was time to take leave— Mr Jones armed me Mr Salisbury, Sophia, & we bade adieu, after passing a very agreeable evening.—

Saturday 23d— Morning walked. Louisa very desirous that I should stay to a little party she was to have in the eveg. so I decided to remain in Chesnut St until Monday. Passed the afternoon entirely alone in the house, & *slept* for want of thought When I was allready to go I found to my no small horror that no carriage had been sent for. There was no one in the house but Mrs Woodward who proposed various desperate measures, one of which was to ask Mrs Chapmans boy to go for one, but as I feared my friend Tommy might think I was summoning him, I negatived that, & after various cogitations remembered that Miss Thacher was going & so sent in by Mrs Woodward to ask her to take me with her— She sent me word that she was going to walk, but that she would call for me. I therefore put myself under her wing & her brothers arm, & we trotted off—

When we arrived found only Louisa, Miss Greenough, & Rutledge in the parlour. And it was long before the rest of the party appeared—there were not more than twelve or fifteen in all. Talked first to Mr Bennet Forbes, who I do not very much admire. Then to Tom Dwight who was very pleasant—while we were talking Mary Minot wailed forth "the old Oak Chest", which is of all the songs I ever *did* hear, the most dismal—[26] Mr Dwight, & I laughed in the most unbecoming manner as the verses preceeded, each more doleful than the former until we arrived at the final catastrophe. After this we had some other songs, & then Mr Jones took Mr Dwights place. He rattled on as usual for the next hour, but I do not remember any thing worth repeating—

the most remarkable incident of the evening was the performance of a short handed orator, by Mr Howard Payne[27] & Mr Jones—Mr Payne making the motions & Mr J making the speech— Mr Payne was *seated* & Mr Jones sat on his lap—a cloak was then thrown round Mr J. which entirely covered Mr Payne, *head* & all.— Mr Paynes arms at no time very long, when hooked on to Mr Jones' person had an effect truly ridiculous, in one hand he brandished a snuff box, & fortunately for his *mouthpiece* the pinches were only imaginary, the motions were very well made tho' absurd in the last degree— Mr Jones made up all manner of nonsense as he went along, & if his sentiments were not pounded into him, it was not the fault of his merciless hands over which he had no control— If laughter was the praise they sought they must have been gratified. I do not remember any other event worth recording— Tom Davis walked home with me. Passed a pleasant evening, tho' the recollection that it was probably the *last* I should ever pass in that house, with Louisa, did not add to my hilarity.[28]

Sunday 24— Went in the morng. to Mr Greenwoods—dined at Mrs Millers—went again in the P.M.—drank tea & passed the eveg at Mrs Parkers.—

Monday 25th Returned to Cambridge— Found I had lost the pleasure of seeing Mr & Mrs Audubon to day, who came to take leave— Mr Audubon however wrote his name in my picture book, which will ever be most valuable to me— In the afternoon drew—do not remember any visitors.

Tuesday 26th Morning Mama & Susan went to town— Sophia & I walked—called at Mrs Higginsons & Mrs Channings, & Susan Higginsons—then walked up to Mr Welles.— Afternoon Mr Frank Gray came— Just come home from Washington with a finished self satisfaction—

Wednesday 27— Morning Mama & Sophia went to town—we drew &c Afternoon Mr Jones called to take leave, but as he returns in two months not many tears were shed— Indeed the *fine edge* of our feelings has been considerably rubbed off by the frequency of these shoccing partings— The device of a pair[29] of scissors, "we part to meet again", should be Mr J's *moto*, though we should not deeply regret did the fatal shears cut the thin spun texture of our friendship. He looked sick, & had we not killed him off in our imaginations so often, might suppose that it was indeed our last meeting but I daresay he will come back to "kill us off" with all possible expedition. I believe he was our only visitor.

Thursday 28th Morning walked— Maria Sedgwick & Miss Pomeroy called to take leave. Afternoon drew. Edward Salisbury our only visitor

Friday 29th. Morning, Mama, Sophia & I went to town, paid various visits—found an invite from Mariann Sullivan for that eveg concluded to stay. [30] Dined at Martha's— Eveg. dressed at Chesnut St: Waited until qtr before nine, for Mary Minot who had promised to call for me at 8 o'ck, then walked with Ed to the door— He was not going, found no one but Tom Dwight in the basement room, which was rather destressing as I wanted some lace *sewed* on to my dress—

There was no woman to take off the things, but hearing a noise in the closet, I thought it might be some of the womankind, therefore approached the door— Whereupon, Mr D was seised with a loud fit of laughter, exclaiming, "Miss Quincy, Mr John Sullivan is in there" Quickly did I retreat, & I presume, that the youth had gone in there upon hearing the bell ring, to arrange some of his attire, the closet fortunately was *dark*, & therefore I had not *ocular* demonstration of the fact, which I conjectured from the glances exchanged by the gentlemen, when Mr S. appeared.— The unfortunate lace was tucked away in despair, & just then Mary & Maria entered.—

We were just ready to go upstairs, when my gloves were no where to be found, a general search commenced but in vain— It was concluded, that I must have either left them at home or dropped them in the street— George Minot offered to go back to Chesnut St to find them, which I gladly accepted— After some time he returned, & fortunately found them on

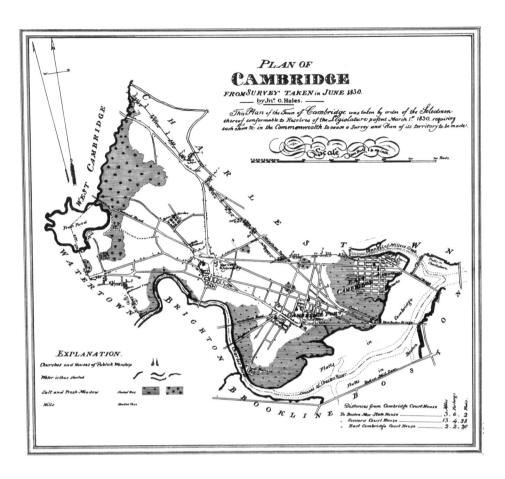

Plan of Cambridge, from a survey taken in June 1830 by Jonathan. G. Hales. This map shows Harvard and the Botanical Garden to the left, and the main road to Boston over the West Boston Bridge to the right. Courtesy of the Cambridge Historical Commission, Cambridge, Mass.

the table at yr house. By this time it was long after nine, an appropriate hour to pay the social *visit* we were invited to. Mr Dwight gave me his arm, & we entered— Very few people there, & they looked as if they had been there so long that they had forgotten that there was a world elsewhere. We at any rate afforded some refreshment to their eyes— Talked some time to Mrs J Amory.— Then had a very pleasant talk with John Sargent— then to Mr Dixwell—

A cotillon was called which I danced with Mr Dixwell— Then Miss Goldsborough sang—disappointed—no sort of expression.— Had a very agreeable talk with D. Russell, who certainly improves more upon a near acquaintance than any of the youths of Boston town— At a distance you think him a conceited, dandified, disagreeable fellow—but as soon as he speaks to you he has so pleasant an expression, has so much to say, & says it so well that you quite change yr opinion— Danced the next dance with him—talked of Europe & of old times, Edward Morse &c &c— By the way, lest I should not mention it, let me here say, that the report we heard last Summer that Mr Morse had been in Boston during that year, was wholly untrue. Mr Russell said he knew it to be entirely unfounded—it was one step beyond even my credulity—tho' heaven knows I have little belief in the gratitude or the memory of man, but I never would credit that Edward Morse[31] would be deficient in common politeness.—

Having given the—Morse his due—I return to the party. Talked the remainer of the eveg to T Dwight—rather stupid.— Mary Minot with whom I was to go away, I saw sailing out of the room entirely forgetting my existance. So I arose & Mr Dwight armed me out—hope Miss Goldsborough did not break her heart.— Had a most ridiculous ride home. Passed "quite" a pleasant eveg.—

Saturday 30th Morning walked up to see Louisa paid her a long visit, then passed an hour in the clutches of Dr Bemis. Then called on Lucilla, & then on Martha. Returned to Chesnut Street about two o'clk On entering the parlour, found ominus signs of a dinner table laid with more than the neat handed Bryants wonted care, & for four persons—Mrs Woodward being heard above, I elevated my voice & desired to know what was the meaning of this apparitition— She informed me that Mr Edmund was going to have two gentlemen to dine with him— I really thought his senses had forsaken him, but as no time was to be lost, I hastely wiped away the honorable dust that collected since your departure—

Soon after Edmund came in & said that the expected visitors were Tom Dwight & T. Davis— It seemed that there was a bet laid by these brother excellencies, Mr Dwight & Mr Quincy, that Mr Dwight would be entrapted into matrimony, (with the help I suppose of his hundred thousands,) before any fair one "noosed" our wary Brother, whose attractions were not so numerous— A dosen of Champagne was pending between these illustrious votaries of the Loves & Graces, which was to be paid to the one who was first sacrificed— Time & the hour, which reveals all things to us common mortals, proved that there is no telling what freaks the little gentleman, "with his bow & arrow" may take in to his head, & in the course of a few months after the bet was laid, a shot from a gentle fair one in Beacon St transfixed the stoney Edmund—for life, while the blushing Tommy was left to pass on, as Mr Vinton *aptly* observed on a similar occasion, "in *maiden* meditation fancy free"! Why the bet had never been paid before, is a mystery, which we *sisters* "who ask no questions" would not be so indiscreet as to enquire, there surely "has been *time* for such a word"— But so it was, my beloved [Flamabella], & as it had been received only a few days before, the gentleman & his friend Mr Davis were invited to drink some of it on this day, as Mr Q. had a lady to set at the head of his table.— I should have thought they would have prefer'd "no incumbrances of that sort", but out of gratitude for the honor of being *allowed* to be critisied by three such quissicalities, I ought to be happy it was so.—

The gentlemen appeared however exceedingly amiable & gallant, & the dinner went off extremely well— Could you have taken a peep, you would certainly have been amused to see E. & me doing the honors— The Champangne was pronounced to be "perfect" & many witty things were said during dinner— Soon after the cloth was removed I vanished to the upper regions,[32] knowing that a speedy retreat is ever considered a most agreeable step in a hostess, & which I hoped might have promoted me to the head of a table in Springfield had not a golden borough stood between me & the Connecticut.— The gentlemen thanked me for honoring their table, & closing the door after me, I saw them no more. Soon after ajourned to Mr Parkers, where Lucilla & I had much amusement as you may suppose, about the dinner party, & then we sat at the window & saw all our ["ken's"] on horse & foot pass in review before us— From the graceful Chaplain, on a prancing steed, down to a plebian peedestrian Wright. Mama & Susan came in to drink tea at Mrs Parkers. I felt dreadfully tired, & played backgammon with Henry all the eveg.— Rode out to C[33] by moonlight bringing Aunt Jackson with us.—

Sunday—31[34] fine day—did not go out in the morning— Mr Wells— Messrs. Kelly Lovering & Dixwell dined here.— Afternoon—Mr Palfrey preached—very good indeed "Love your enemies"— In the eveg Mr Minot & Josiah came out—also Mr Coggswell, Mr Chaplain, Mr Felton, Mr Wigglesworth, Messrs. King & Ellis— were our visitors <*a page was cut out and some letters are written on the cut page in the remaining left margin, e.g. D(ixwell), P(alfrey), F(elton])*> Mr Chaplain was as usual all elegance. And was more

animated, than I have seen him for some time—less astray and absent—
He is in general thought silent and haughty, and I do not wonder at his
being so considered— There are times when he is himself, when he can
be "all our fancy painted him"—and he then combines "much that we are
apt to like" in one so gifted in ~~all~~ outward advantages—but there is still
something very strange about him, this even I am forced to allow.— The
other gentlemen seemed to be agreeable. The faithful Felton looked uncommonly well, and certainly is "an excellent person"—barring the Kent
mystery. We passed a very agreeable evening—books & pictures flying
about as usual.—

CHAPTER 2

Fanny Kemble's Boston Appearance

April 1833

Attending a theatrical performance of Fanny Kemble (in *The Hunchback* on 13 May), Anna Quincy wrote, "Fanny Kemble I thank you for the pleasure— & the pain you have given me— You will be long remembered." The diary for this period graphically reflects pleasure and pain, Anna's reactions to the acclaimed actress.

"Sensational" is not too strong an adjective for the American tour of the British actress Frances Anne Kemble, later Butler (1809–93), and her father, Charles Kemble (1775–1854) in 1832–34. Fanny Kemble had made her debut in London in 1829 hoping to restore the Kemble family's declining fortunes. She became an immediate success. Carrying her fame lightly, she mixed easily with the most esteemed British literati. In America she was wildly celebrated; horses and flowers were named after her.[1]

After a triumphal run in New York, Philadelphia, and Washington, D.C., father and daughter performed in Boston from 16 April until 17 May 1833. Reviewing Miss Kemble in Shakespeare's *Much Ado about Nothing*, the *Boston Evening Transcript* critic wrote: "It is said that her genius which glowed so brilliantly in Bianca [*Fazio*] and Juliet, was restrained in the character of Beatrice. It was not so. On the contrary, her genius was made to exhibit itself in a widely different field, and yet came off triumphant." The tragedy *Fazio*, written by Henry Hunt Milman, was so popular that extra performances were arranged. Although Anna compliments Bostonians for their restrained reception of the Kembles (see 17 April entry), by contrast the *Boston Daily Advertiser* critic wryly commented that "the Kemble Fever has not turned yet—the doctors are in constant attendance, however, and convalescence is anticipated soon."[2]

Fanny Kemble also commented on the Boston crowds demanding tickets for performances; on 17 April she wrote of the "yelling and shouting" at the Tremont Theatre box office as people sought tickets for *The Stranger*: "In they rush, thumping and pummelling one another, and not one comes out without rubbing his head, or his back, or showing a piteous rent in his clothes." Yet she later described her stay in Boston as "delightful. . . . The people are intellectual, and have been most abundantly good-natured and kind to me."[3]

In her autobiographical notes, Anna Quincy Waterston reminisced on her theatergoing in the 1820s and 1830s; it had been a part of her life since early childhood. She had seen the British actor William Macready (1793–1853) portray Shakespeare's Hamlet when she was fifteen and the rising American star Edwin Forrest (1806–72) in *Venice Preserved*. Anna's interest in the lively arts continued with her biography of the opera singer Adelaide Phillips, whose career she encouraged.[4]

Yet to Anna the theater in those early days was full of "improprieties": she wrote, "hardly a place for decent [women]." Young women should avoid the "pit," where sat men of the "lowest" class, as well as "the upper gallery [which] was filled with women of the worst character." She recalled her mother's advising that from her vantage point of the box, "not to look up or down—at gallery or pit."[5] With its comment that the theater is "no fit place for an elegant female," Anna's entry for 30 April illustrates these "improprieties."

She wrote her farewell tribute to Fanny Kemble on 13 May in an emotional outpouring:

> The fixed and yearning looks of strong affection
> The actioned turmoil of a bosom rending
> When pity, love, and honour are contending;—
> Who have beheld all this, I ween!
> A lovely, grand, and wondrous sight have seen.

Public weeping might seem embarrassing, as Anna wrote on 16 April after seeing Kemble as Bianca in *Fazio*, but it was a fitting response to the famed actress. Anna's feelings were echoed by the general lamentations of 18 May, when the Kembles departed Tremont House, Boston's most elegant hotel. The *Boston Evening Transcript* observed: "About ten o'clock, never were so many sad pretty faces seen together in that one small space between Beacon and Park street corners: the sun blazed fervently upon their heads, as they were stretched from the windows to catch a last, lingering look."[6]

Accompanied by such fanfare, small wonder that Fanny Kemble's Boston tour made such a strong impression on Anna Quincy.

April 1833

Monday 1 April Heard at breakfast the melancholy tidings of Mr Ashmuns death[7]— We heard last eveg. that he was ill, but had no idea that the closing scene was so near— His health has been so wretched, that we ought not to regret his release for his own sake—but 33, seems an early age to give up a life so useful—& so valuable— Mr Ashmun had no idea that he was more ill last evening than he often had been, and had made all his arrangements to go to Concord, the next day, to attend some cause in which he was engaged— before that day arrived he had been summoned to another bar—where we cannot but believe that his useful & irreproachable life, will receive the reward, which was unfinished on Earth.— The day being a beautiful one, we took a pleasant drive to Mt Auburn, &c &c— Miss Lowell (Grandma's friend) dined here.— Mr & Mrs Farrar—& A Whitney in the eveg.

Tuesday 2d— Drew &c Mr Chaplain called, passed an hour in looking over Audubon's great book—&c. very pleasantly. In the afternoon Mary Jane J—Josiah—Mr Dearborn & Bond came. Evening H Cleveland.

Wednesday 3d— Morning walked. Mr Church came, as "jolly" as ever— Informed us he was coming out to Cambridge next week to join the Law school— Alas—what is a church, if we must lose our Chaplain— This is indeed "taking the money & leaving the box",—but so it is my beloved [Flamabella]. In the afternoon, Mama, Sophia & I went in to town— S. & I to attend Mr Paynes benefit. Took up our rest again in Chesnut Street—. While Edmund, Sophy & I were taking a social cup in the parlour—a ring at the door announced Mr Chaplain, who was to be of the party,— So you see, we are not content with giving dinner parties in yr absence, but forsooth must have tea drinkings also.— We may come to a Ball before yr return— The youth however positively decline the cup of kindness, & only joined in our social "chat", until 7 o'ck, when the carriage came to the door, & we departed— Stopt for Louisa in Park St—who appeared attended by Rutledge.

We then proceeded to the Theatre. Mr Forbes, had arranged the most fashionable portion of the company in the 2d Row, which was a mistake I think. He recd us at the box door, & in we all scrambled. The house was not a full one by any means, but very respectable, & the Ladies, were most elegantly arrayed— Our box was a very pretty one, I mean the ladies in it, & all the ladies looked better than I ever saw them at the Theatre. The first play had commenced when we came in, & as, from where we were perched we could neither see nor hear, we talked thro' the whole of it. At the end thereof, Sophia finding she was half crushed, exceedingly warm, & moreover observing as she said, that she kept all the beaux, from talking to the hapless Louisa, with great kindness to her (I am sure in this instance virtue met its own reward), decided to seek a more agreeable seat below, & vanished with Edmund, & I soon saw her agreeably established in the box next the stage, with Mrs Shaw— The heat upstairs was beyond

OPPOSITE: Plan of the City of Boston. Most of the homes Anna visited were close to Boston Common: the Millers on Park Street, the Minots and Parkers on Beacon Street, and the Salisburys and Grants on Mt. Vernon Street. The Quincys' city residence on Chesnut Street is one block to the right of Beacon Street. From the Boston City Directory, 1832–1833, courtesy of the Massachusetts Historical Society.

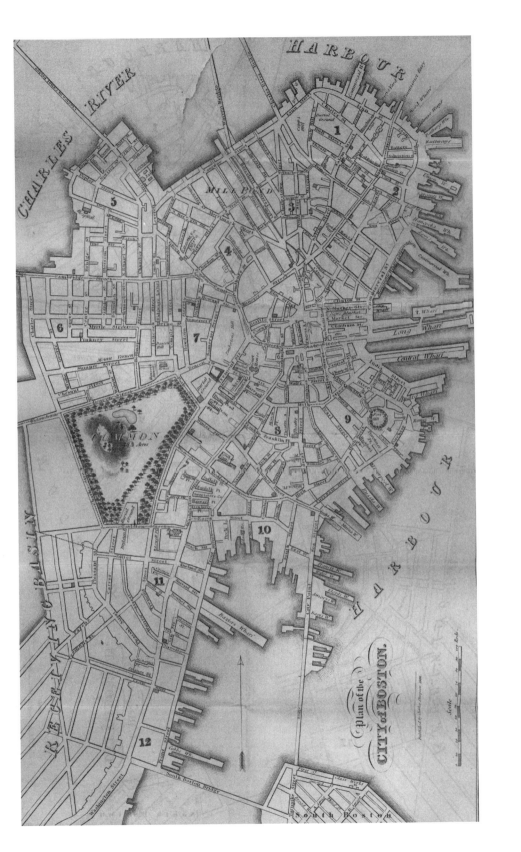

Plan of the
CITY of BOSTON.

description, & I had nothing but an ivory fan that was entirely useless— Mr Chaplain declared that he would go in search of a better one, & notwithstanding all I could say, rushed from the box, & in a short time returned bearing in his hand a large feather fan, which he said he had found in a drawer at the Tremont House— To this most useful deed of gallantry, I am sure we were indebted, that we ever left the box without being entirely melted.

Between the plays, all the agreeable beaux vibrated.[8] Mr T Dwight looking "as bright as a button" Mr D. Russell, exceeding animated & agreeable. Mr Joseph Lyman, handsome & pleasing Mr Wolcott ditto, ditto, and various others equally worthy of honorable mention.— One, or two other pieces were performed tolerably—but really there was no judging from the top of creation where we were perched. An address written by Mr Park Benjamin in honor of Mr Payne was then spoken, by Mrs Barrett— It was very prettily written indeed, & concluded with some appropriate welcome to his "own sweet Home" whereupon the orchestra burst forth in the air of "Sweet Home"[9]— (I was wicked enough to think of Mrs [Lum]) which had a pretty effect. Mr Payne was then called for, & at length made his appearance— Went through the usual ceremonies of bowing, laying his hand on his heart "& turning all manner of colours"— his address however was too long, & rather bewildering, as at some parts the audience, were some what at a loss to know what he was driving at, however we will not be too critical.

After this came "the Lancers" which was the best acting, merely a little interlude. The heroine of the play was named *Louisa Marston*, & as Mr Forbes informed me, actually named by Mr Payne after the *real* Louisa Marston, who he used to know & admire in former days.— I was seated between Mr Forbes & Mr Chaplain, and should have had a pleasant time, had not Mr Forbes, been in a perfect fidget about the thinness of the house, &c &c He poor man, had taken great interest, great trouble & expense about it, & seemed to be provoked & mortified at its want of success—& had not diplomacy enough to "smile & smile & be a villain" & say nothing about it[10]— He kept pouring his woes into my ear, until I really felt so disagreab[le] that I wished him, at least one box off.—

On the other side, my fate at the end of the eveg, was not much better—for the hapless Chaplain, who had been riding a hard trotting horse the whole afternoon, (which if we could judge from his appearance when we saw him pass through Cambridge soon after dinner, could not be "imagined for an instant to be a bed of Roses") was so dreadfully fatigued that by the time the *fourth* piece commenced, he really seemed to be unable to support existence, & was almost deprived of the powers of speech, & I really expected to have a *fainting* Leicester to weep over.— Knowing that he intended riding out to Cambridge that night on the same "*vil animal*", I begged him to depart immediately & as we had other gentleman with us, not to think himself obliged to stay any longer—

Sophia & I who were "tired to death", would have been thankful to go also, but the fair Louisa was evidently unwilling to depart, & we did not like to oblige her to do so.— After many apologies for so shocking a piece of ungallant conduct our "*wearied Hope*", took leave, & having thus despatched one of my forlorn swains, & endeavoured to turn a deaf ear to the Forbes wailings, I tried to listen to what was going on, on the stage.

There was an immense pause before the last play, which at length commenced. It was Charles 2d— the same one we saw acted the Lafayette night—but did not seem at all *like* the same— We decided to beat a retreat as soon as the first act was over, & while we were yet speaking the box door opened & in came Mr Chaplain, who I had imagined safe at Cambridge, & half through his first sleep. But it appeareth, that our fatigued friend had searched in vain for the gallant steed, which truely seemed to be the "rock" destined to "*rack the hapless lover*" on this eventful day, and had searched with out success. Whether some brother Southerner who had been forced "to drink his own horses"[11] had conveyed it away to the classic shades, or what had become of it, must be classed with many other mysteries that gather round the Chaplain history, but the result was before us, & the youth returned just in time to cloak the ladies & attend them to their carriage.— The whole party were pretty well done up—but we were all glad that we had gone & done all in our power to aid Mr Payne, & his dispairing Patron Mr Forbes.—

Thursday 4th Returned to Cambridge immediately after breakfast.— A year from to day we sat off on our eventful tour "to the South"[12] — No one came I believe.—

Friday 5th Morng— Rec: Abbys letter from Baltimore— Afternoon attended the Eulogy upon Mr Ashmun, in the Chapel.— It was an extremely interesting scene— the Chapel was very well filled & by the most respectable audience— Many of the distinguished Lawyers, from Boston, & many of the young gentlemen who had been formerly under Mr Ashmuns care— The body was placed in the centre aisle, & I could not but remember that the last time we were assembled on a public occasion in the Chapel, (the dedication of the Dane Law College) Mr Ashmun occupied that very place— The services were opened by an appropriate Hymn, which was well sung, then followed a very fine prayer by Mr Palfrey, which was very eloquent & interesting. The following lines were then sung, which I copy as being very appropriate, altho' I dare say you have often read them.

> Oh what is man, great Maker of Mankind,!
> That Thou to him so great respect should bear!
> That Thou adorn'st him with so bright a mind
> Makes Him a Kings, & e'en an Angels peer.

> Oh! what a lively life, what Heavenly power
> What spreading virtue, what a sparkling fine
> How great, how plentiful, how rich a dower
> Dost Thou within this dying flesh inspire.
> Nor hast thou given these blessings for a day
> Nor made them on the bodys life depend
> The soul, though made in Time, survives for ay,
> And though it both beginning, sees no end.—

Judge Storys Eulogy was very interesting & just what it ought to have been. It was simple & <a page cut off has a few letters in the left margin that appear to be from an earlier entry> without being extravagant & touching without being at all commonplace.—

Mr Ashmun must certainly have been a most uncommon man—to have risen at the early age of thirty-three to the first rank of his profession—notwithstanding many disadvantages & that most trying one, constant ill health— His mind seemed to rise above all impediments, & while he lived he excerted its powers to their utmost, & to the very last— His death was sudden at the end—tho' long expected— He died with perfect tranquillity & seemed to pass from one state of existence to another almost without an interruption to his usefulness.— The services were concluded, by the anthem "Unveil thy bosom, faithful tomb"—which was very sweetly sung[13]— The men then came forward to remove the body— Several of Mr. Ashmuns pupils, as if moved by an irresistable impulse, pressed forward and surrounded him for the last time. They were to see his face no more—

"For the stares of science brought them
For the charm his goodness gave
For the lessons he had taught them
They could give him—but a grave"—

It was a very touching scene—and one which I shall never forget. The funeral then proceeded to Mt Auburn where Mr. Ashmun was interred—His tomb is on the very summit of Harvard Hill, which commands a beautiful distant view of Cambridge—& which seems to be a most appropriate resting place, for one so excellent in life— Dr Shattuck presented the University with this place which he had previously bought for himself, but which he thought particularly appropriate to this and all other similar occasions. [14]— In the eveg Papa set off on his journey.—

Saturday 6— Mama went to Dedham &c

Sunday 7th Forget what we did.—

Monday 8th Easterly Storm notwithstanding which, Mrs [D] Hoffman of Baltimore, her son, & Mr F. Gray came— Mrs Hoffman is ladylike & pleasing—young Mr H, coming to enter College. Eveg Read loud in Persuasion, which is certainly the most natural thing you can possibly imagine. [15]—

Tuesday 9th drew &c Do not remember any visitors—

Wednesday 10 Morning— Susan & I called on Mrs Sparks, who is established at Mrs Cragies in the apartment which a Hutchinson deigned to <a printed tribute to John Ashmun, pasted in here, obscures the text on the left side> "grace", for so many summers. [16] It looked to be sure rather different being new furnished &c Mrs Sparks is quite pleasing, but nothing very [??]tra— After a visit to her, we took up Sophia [??] went to Town. First called at Mrs Parkers, then Susan & I called on Mrs Hoffman at [??] Tremont. Found her at home—looking [ve]ry pretty— She is a very fair specimen of the [S]outhern ladies—pretty, delicate, quite artificial, yet quite attractive in her manners— Paid her a long visit, & after leaving cards at various other mansions, where the welcome sound of "not at home" saluted our ears, drove to Miss Rings—

Here some convenient shoe being loose, Horace departed to call for us again in a few moments— Susan & I went to various shops, & met various people, with whom as usual Susan had everlasting colloquies— Just as I was in a *gentle* manner expostulating with her, lo!—as is often the case, we are tempted to do the very thing ourselves which we reprimand in others— For who should heave in sight at that moment, but Leut Thomas Adams.[17]— Gracefully advancing, "in shawl drapery", I extended my hand, and mutual recognition—followed & the questions "when are you going away" & "how long have you been here", were more gently insinuated than it has *always* been the youths fate to hear them. He informed us he was just departing for *Pittsburg*— Had been here some time, "muttered something about butter & oranges" & regret at not having *been able* to call at *Cambridge*— I wonder what hindered him—but concealing my feelings I wished him health & happiness—& waving our heads we parted—and I "watched the morning light play around his fine figure" until an envious baggage waggon shut it from my sight. I must not forget that Mr Adams enquired after Mrs Greene, & wished to know where she was, & hoped that it was possible that he might meet her.

After this tender scene, I got in to the carriage, & then joined Susan at Miss Bents. Elisabeth Grant was then seen at the door, & I requested her to get in & have a social chat, while I waited for Susan— In she came, & to it we went— the first intelligence she gave me was, that the faithless Vinton had taken his *final departure* "with out so much as saying thank-ee", for all we have sacrificed to detain him— Et tu Brute "But men were deceivers ever" and if even the gallantry of "the *Officers*", which has held so high a rank in our estimation, is thus proved to be indeed but "a butterfly state", we almost give up all hopes of the age of chivalry— But "I'll keep my heart another day", in the hope that the shadow of chivalry—politeness, yet adorns the noble Leicester— Should he too prove that "friendships balmy words but feign" we shall be forced to exclaim with Sir Peter Teasle "This is a—wicked world we live in, and the fewer we praise in it the better."[18]—

After having discussed this interesting topic to our satisfaction, I asked Elisabeth to let us set her down wherever she was going—as she looked pale, & perfectly fagged— (Not that I add'd *that* to my invitation) as she had been hunting the whole morning, not after happiness, but after a pair of long gloves, not a pair of which was to had for love or money in Boston. According we drove to Whitatakers,[19] where we parted— Susan & I went to Cousin Susans & then taking up Sophia, returned to Cambridge.— Mrs Guild, Cousin N. Storer & Harriot & Charles came— Evg—finished Persuasion,— & felt as if we could not bear to part with Anne Elliot & Capt Wentworth

Thursday 11th Morning drew— Afternoon Sophia & I went to town—

at attend a party at Miss Pickerings. Went over to see Mary Minot. Saw Mrs M— had an account of Williams accident, & all the various ills that had befallen them, but which Mrs Minot seemed to bear with her usual philosophy— Staid there some time—then returned to Chesnut Street. About 9 Sophy & I went to Miss Pickerings— The first cotillon was dancing when we entered— Talked to Mr Bassett, who is extremely agreeable. The next cotillon to my amusement up stept Mr Gardner (the divinity student) & asked me to dance—which accordingly I did— Made out better than I expected, & with the exception of some odd hopping & skipping did very well— His likeness to Quincy M—is really tormenting. It seems almost to be the same person. Mr Wolcott was my next partner—looked handsome—"but wants to me the witching grace" of elegance, without which there can be little real beauty in man or woman— Mr Robbins, & J O Sargent were the next—

John Codman, then came up & asked me to go to Supper with him, so leaving Geo: Minot to find some other partner for the next dance, we ascended a *steep* staircase, affording to the world below a knowledge that we had good *understandings* & reached the Library, where was a table— Here we passed some time very agreeably. My friend Johnny, being very pleasant we then returned to the dancing room, & joined the next dance with Geo: Minot, then with Mr Brewster, Mr [Isavernie]—a real oddity a half Greek—& *whole Jew*, who I knew in New York— Then with Mr Donaldson, & then took our departure— Howard Sargent gave me his arm & we went upstairs & while we were putting on our things he sits down on the bed, in the take off room, in a happy state of absence of mind, which I presume prevented him from perceiving the absurdity thereof.— The music was perfectly exquisite, the peices selected with great taste, & the tunes they played—perfectly delightful. Sophia passed an amusing evening, & it seemed to be an animated one. There were a good many people I did not know—& odd looking men, of every shape & sise, many of whom I believe were collegians as they continually bowed to us—tho' who they were we could not imagine.—

Friday 12th Went up to see Martha, paid her a long visit—then went Mrs Minots— Saw Mary all on the mending line, & seemed almost free from apprehension on William's account.— Sophia & I bringing out Miss Storrow then drove out to Cambridge.—

Saturday 13th Forgot what we did—nothing very remarkable.—

Sunday 14th Morning went to church— Mr Stetson preached a very fine sermon, but his immensity is absolutely horrific. Mr S. dined here— Afternoon staid at home— Edmund & Mr Wells the eveg visitors.—

Monday 15— fine day— Decided to drive over to the Plains to see Mrs Russell— While we were dressing, young Mr Hoffman & Frank Schroeder came— I was not aware of their being in the house, & entered the parlour just as they were exiting, which made a charming somerset at the door— After an affectionate shake of the hand—(men, I had no glove on) the young gentlemen returned to the parlour— Mr Schroeder, who left Cambridge about two years since, a delicate, modest, tho' handsome boy now stood before us, a finished gentleman, fresh from the best schools of dandism that New York & Phila afford,—armed at all points, but having from the appearance of ill health, lost much of his beauty— He returns to join the Law school Cambridge, being a good *nominal* residence & an excellent place to set out from— Fortunately our "elegant beasts" are never examined as to the amount of their attainments, or I fear that "many good things in Law" would be indeed found wanting— The young gentlemen remained until the carriage came to the door —& assisted us in,—& took leave—

We then drove to the Plains & after much driving to & fro—& stoppings at divers places, at length found Mrs Russells lodgings— Mrs R. & Louisa were at home— The place not at all pleasant & altogether the scene is indeed changed. The elegant, the gay, the fashionable, not to say extravagant Mrs Russell, banished to this small & comfortless lodging in the country— It is indeed no small trial & the knowledge that it is in consequence of her own imprudence, can give her but little satisfaction. Mrs R. looked sick & unhappy—Louisa, bright & pretty—but the change is a sad one to her & the visit by no means a pleasant one. After it was over, drove thro' town— Stopt at Josiahs office & then at Mrs Millers— The City looked delightful— Stopt a moment at Mrs. Parkers & then returned to Cambridge.—

Tuesday 16th Sophia & I went in to town— Went first to Mr Parkers— found that they had been the evening before to see Kemble in Hamlet— Miss K's first appearance was to be this evening, & I "was wild" to see her— Every thing of course in true *star* confusion about the tickets. All things uncertain, but if possible determined to go to the Theatre first & then to a party at Mrs Harry Otis'. Sophia waited in town in hopes of finding Papa arrived, but no stages came in, & there the hapless child remained all day in her hat & cloak a victim to uncertainties. As the day wore on, & nothing was heard of the Tickets I began to give up all hopes of them— However thought I would dress for Mrs Otis' before Sophia went out of town, & lucky it was I did so—for just as I was ready, and at nearly ½ past six—Josiah flew in & said he had 3 tickets in No 5— This was delightful, & at a little before 7, Susan Josiah & I drove to the Theatre— We were just in time, & found excellent seats—

The play was "Fasio" or "the Italian wife" a tragedy of the deepest kind with much stage effect tho' miserably written— When the Curtain drew up, Bianca, & Fazio—(Mr & Miss Kemble) were discovered at a table.— A thunder of applause from an over flowing house greeted her—& three times three, was given to the graceful *bendings* of the fair Stranger. The play then commenced.— The story is briefly this— Bianca & Faiso are husband & wife, extremely happy—tho' poor—until Faiso is tempted by the opportune murder of an old miser, to take possession of the said old misers property, without any right to it.— This immense wealth of course raises them to the highest rank, & brings Faiso in to the sphere of the Lady Aldebella, "who is no better than she should be,"[20] tho' of very high rank— Bianca with extremely good reason, becomes dread-fully jealous & distressed, & while in a perfect agony of love & jealousy hears that the Duke, (the Governor of the state) is searching for the murderer of the old miser— Bianca, is the only person who knows that it was by robbing this miser, that Fasio became so wealthy, but knows also, that he did not murder him. In a fit of dispair, she determines to go, to the Duke & betray her husbands secret, & in that way to get him out of Aldebellas power. The moment the thought occurs she rushes to the Duke, & tells the story— Fasio, is immediately summoned—clears himself from the murder—but confesses the Robbery—& is condemned to death before Biancas' face— who as you may suppose is now filled with horror dispair & agony—at being the murderer of her husband to whom of course, she is most devotedly attached— She strives in every way to save him— Even goes to Aldebella & entreats her to save his life & even tells her that if she will but save him, she will give him up forever, & that he shall be Aldebellas— Aldebella, however spurns the idea, & secretly rejoices that his death may prevent her character being known— Fasio is executed, & Bianca rushes in to Aldebellas *ball room* distracted—& dies on the stage—commending her children to the Duke—!!

The play was one admirably calculated to show off Miss Kemble, who entirely equalled—indeed passed my expectations— Her grace—the

expression of her countenance—her *shrieks*, her starts—are admirable—
Her voice has rather too much stage *tone*, but there are tones of it which
went to my heart. Her great power however is in her attitudes, & her expression—& her *laugh* of agony & insanity was truly horrific. The moment
which I think produced most effect on the house, was at the moment
when Fasio is to be led off to execution in the prison— She has just been
imploring the Jailor to delay a few moments, in the most passionate manner, when the bell tolls—the sound of which seemed to turn her into marble— She stood riveted to the spot— Her eyes fixed, her cheek pale as
ashes. Fasio embraces her, but she is entirely insensible of it—& he is led
off the stage, leaving her the solitary figure,— She stood, I should think
five moments—a perfect statue—and the deathlike stillness that reigned
over the crowded audience, every person seeming to hold their breath—
was very striking— "She stood the bloodless image of despair"[21] until the
bell tolled again—at that sound the full sense of her wretchedness
[seemed] to rush upon her mind—and nearly to destroy it— She gave a
start, which every one seemed to feel, & with one of her thrilling screams
of agony rushed from the stage.

It was a most tremendous affair altogether, & altho' I did my best to
hold up my head like a person of fashion & to conceal my tender feelings,
it was in vain, & the more I tried the more I cried,— Miss Hodgkinson
who sat next to me, was even more overset— She is quite intimate with
Miss Kemble, having come out in the same ship with her from England.— It was the first time however, she had ever seen her on the stage,
& if it had been her own sister she could not have seemed more deeply interested in her.— When the curtain fell—Miss H. & I turned our weeping
glance on each other—& neither could resist a smile at the idea of our
being fit to be seen at Mrs Otis—

However, as Bianca herself was to be there, we determined to go— Exchanging a few half smothered expressions of our "*tearful joy*" we prepared
to leave the box— John Codman came to the box door, & gave ~~me~~ his arm
to the weeping fair one,— I was almost ashamed that he—or any one
should see how much I was affected, & did my best to stop my tears—
which however were flowing in full force, when we stopt at Mrs Otis'
Door— We remained in the take off room until I looked rather less frightful, but I fear did not shine that evening—

Susan & I then desended—Josiah being with us—found the room
filled with the usual variety of an Otis party—Miss Kemble of course the

universal topic— Talked to Leut Sawyer—Mr Miers, Mr [Isavernie], &c
&c—but remember nothing worth repeating—went into the other room
with Mr Sawyer—talked to that wise acre, Mr Church— by the way, I must
relate a good play upon his name which Mama made the other day— I
was regretting that those who were going to leave Cambridge, & those
who were *coming*, could not change places— "To be sure" said Mama "it
is sad that the Chaplain is going to leave us nothing but an *empty
Church*"— "Good" was it not—but I must return to the party. Mr Church
introduced some friend to me, a handsome, but uninteresting youth, but
if yr future happiness depends upon knowing his name I fear in my heart,
it is blighted, for like Betty Williams I only know it began with a B. but
whether a *bumble* B—or a *honey* B—I know not—

With Mr B I went back into the other room, & found that Miss Kemble
had arrived. I however could not then catch a glimpse of her the crowd
round her being *dense*—not *over* civil it appeared to me— For tho' accustomed to be the object of general attention, it must be a very different
thing, being stared at in a private party, where she appears as a young
Lady, & where on the Stage— She was sitting down in a window close to
the door where she entered, appearing extremely modest & unassum-
ing—and I could hardly believe that this delicate, gentle, subdued *shadowy* creature, was the Bianca, who had been exhibiting such power, &
who had made me feel so much.—

Mr Kemble is a fine looking man —very much of a gentleman & very
little of the actor about him— Miss Kemble drops the character of Actress
entirely, & tho' doubtless her manner in company is one of her fine pieces
of *acting*, still she chooses her part well—& plays it with good effect— Towards the end of the evening when there was hardly anyone near her— I
went to speak to Miss Hodgkinson, who was standing by her— She introduced me to Miss Kemble, as I wanted to see her & was not up to *staring*
without speaking— We exchanged a few commonplaces—but her voice
was so low, that I could hardly hear a word she said— She is not handsome off the stage. She has very fine eyes with very black eyelashes & eyebrows—& fine teeth—her complexion is coarse, & her other features not
remarkable[22]— her head is well shaped—& hair dressed like Mrs
Cobb's—who, by the way, I think she resembles a little— She appeared
like any other young lady—but had a very intelligent expression when she
spoke.—

We were very glad to have an opportunity of seeing her off the stage, &

were very agreeably impressed— Soon after this took leave— John Codman went to the carriage with me, & I was glad to show him, that I could "wipe away my tears" [23]— The party was quite a pleasant one—but I had been so wrought up by the play, that I could hardly come down to the common places of a party & beaux & nonsense. Returned to Chesnut Street.

Wednesday 17th Went to Mrs Parkers soon after breakfast— Talked over the past evening & made arrangements to go again this eveg to see "the Stranger" Mrs Haller being one of Miss Kembles finest characters.— Called at Mrs Salisburys—Mrs Minots &c— Found tickets arrived for the eveg— Edmund had been to call on the fair Fanny—& was much pleased with her & her father— The Bostonians, however, have behaved just right about these people. Have not got in to the fever they did, about Macready, but tho' much delighted, & filling crowded houses, have not been at all distracted.— In the afternoon Sophia came in to go—to the Theatre— heard also that Papa was safe at home, after a delay of one day, by some accident to the boat.

7 o'ck again found us in No 5—at the Theatre. Mary Jane—Josiah, Lucilla, Miss Tidmarsh, Sophia Edmund & myself— House again crowded & fashionable. Soon after the play began— Mary Jane discovered to her horror that she had forgot her *pocket handkerchief*—& of all articles—a handkerchief is the most necessary in beholding "the Stranger"— What was to be done?— To wipe away the tears of tragedy with a *pair* of gloves was indeed dreadful— I offered her *half* of mine, well knowing that I should need it all—but of course, she could not take it—& Josiah's *silk one*, was almost as unsentimental as the gloves— In this dilemma, I applied to the other Ladies & found to our satisfaction that the provident Sophia, had brought two—Remembering *Douglas*.[24]— This was a relief & all went on—

You I believe saw Macready in "the Stranger," & will remember that is really heartrending— Mr Kemble performed the stranger very well— The other characters were very well supported, and Mrs Haller, particularly in the last scenes—was admirable—and so touching was it, that it drew "iron tears" down the cheeks even of the men in the pit— Many of the gentlemen wept, & those who did not were as pale as ashes.— I need say nothing about *the Ladies* — they were nearly *dissolved*— I never saw a house more universally affected, through the vain attempts to disguise it, with ominous *snuffling*, & applications of white handkerchiefs[25]—

The last scene, was really too much—where the Stranger forgives—
but forever parts, with Mrs Haller— Their children are brought in, & her
shriek of agony at the sight of them was really electric— She then falls
prostrate at her husbands feet, & the Curtain drops— The handerchiefs
were then doubly useful—& the tears we shed were almost more than
ought to be wasted on imaginary sorrows— Mary Jane & I were utterly deprived even of the power of speaking—& only exchanged a weeping
glance at each other— Mr Chaplain appeared at the box door—but not
even Mr Chaplain could check the briney tears—& for my life I could not
speak a word in reply to his enquiries as to how I was pleased &c.

Seeing my forlorn state of mind he politely desisted from talking, &
gave me his arm, to support my trembling steps— Edmund had the other
ladies under his protection & when we reached the door, he consigned
the four weeping damsels to Mr Chaplains care, while he went to find the
carriage, tho' in the agitation of the moment Edmund entirely forgot Mr
C's name and with various wavings of the hand & repetitions of Mr. was
obliged to leave it unremembered.— We were at last safely deposited in
the carriage—& drove to Mr Parkers where we left Lucilla & Miss Tidmarsh & took up Susan, bag & baggage, & sped out to Cambridge—

We of course had been much delighted with the evening— "Call it but
pleasure and the pill goes down" for under other circumstances to have
passed two evenings in weeping & shrieking would be deemed an odd way
of being amused and really does it not seem ridiculous to go to be made
to feel miserable— It adds much to the pleasure of seeing Miss Kemble to
see her supported by her father which takes away every thing that is disagreeable— I am very sorry that you did not see her in tragedy, which is
the only part she ought to take— She dislikes Comedy herself, & says she
can not enter into it—& I do not wonder at yr being disappointed in her,
when you saw her in Phila but I think were you to see one of her fine trag-
ic characters you would admire her as much as we do.—

Thursday 18th Walked— Mr & Mrs Bethune called to take leave— Mrs
Hoffman & young Hoffman Miss Barber & Miss Duncan, were the other
morning visitors— Mr & Mrs Guild, Elisabeth Harrot, Charles, & Anna
Ticknor dined here, had quite a pleasant day—played all manner of
things with the children till we nearly fell down— Mrs Blake, Miss Bruce,
& Miss Blake, came in the afternoon. Mrs Dwight & Anna D. also dropt
in—as did like wise Miss Storrow— This being one of those days when
every body sets out to come. The Guild party staid till after tea. In the

evening Mr Gardner & Mr Phipps came. We were some what fatigued, & neither of our visitors possessing much flow of conversation, it was rather draging— Mr Gardner however sang delightfully. Particularly, "my boy Tammy" which is an exquiste little thing, & he sings it with a taste & feeling worthy of the sweetness of a Scotch ballad.

Friday 19th Drew all the morning— Mrs Minot Mrs Sedgwick, & Mrs Channing—Mr Hoffman & Mr Wells came— Afternoon & eveg drew &c— forget what we did in the eveg.—

Saturday 20 Mama & I went to Dedham— Had a very pleasant drive— Passed the day quite pleasantly with Aunt Dowse. Returned home through town & did not reach home until quite late.—

Sunday 21— did not go to church in the morng. Mr Wells—Mssrs. Harrington & Whitney, & Horace Cleveland dined here— Went to church in the P.M— Mr Putnam of Roxbury preached, very interesting indeed.— Josiah & Edmund came out to tea. In the evening Mr & Mrs Farrar—Mr Chaplain, Mr Schroeder, Mr Feton & Dr Beck, were the visitors. We passed quite a pleasant one—discussed Miss Kemble with Mr Chaplain, together with various other interesting topics— The youth looked hand-some & elegant, but has lost much of his beauty, & the baneful air of the City has sadly dimmed "his original brightness";[26] Mr Schroeder was as captivating as usual, and is entirely in the "sweet line". Affects the most delicate timid childlike manners, & seems to solicit the interest of every one he addresses, to treat with kindness one so young & so inexperi-enced— This pretty affectation is really well supported, & is well suited to his delicate appearance, and almost feminine beauty.— The young gen-tlemen paid an agreeable visit & after their excit, talked to Mr Felton— who was indeed a contrast to the fair & refined Schroeder. We shouted as usal at imaginary wit, but I do not remember any thing very well worth re-peating.—

Monday 22d— Had the pleasure of receiving yr first letter from Char-lotte—which was indeed welcome, as we had not heard from you for three weeks. In the afternoon, Mrs Hoffman & Mr Frank Gray came—Mrs H. to take leave.—

Tuesday 23d.— Morng— Received Abbys letter from Charlotte, with which we were greatly amused.— In the afternoon Sophia & I went to town. In the eveg went to a party at Mrs T. W. Wards for Miss Kemble.[27] It was a very handsome party indeed— Carpet up in one room very good music—but a dreadful dearth of beaux— Miss Kemble looked remarkably handsome— there is something exceedingly striking in her face— it is one of those that haunt you after you have seen it—like some Sibyl, or enchantress— I do not know whether it is an agreeable expression, but nothing can be finer than her large black eyes, or more expressive than her flexible mouth. Her frame is very muscular, and seems made to express the strongest emotions. She is grace personified, & her dancing was perfection—Uniting great skill, & animation with perfect grace & ladylike deportment. She is indeed a creature gifted most highly and I should think deserved what has been said of her that "she is the most remarkable woman of the age".— Mr Kemble was very much fatigued by the part he had been performing, & they staid but a very short time, which was not over & above civil—considering the party was made for her.— We passed quite an amusing eveg.—

Wednesday 24— Returned to Cambridge— Intended to have gone to the Theatre—but the play being "Venice Preserved" we could not muster up sufficient *brass* to attend.[28]

Thursday 25th Morng Mama & I went to town—paid various visits— but saw no one except Mrs Ticknor & Mrs Salisbury.— Afternoon drew— Evening Mr Hoffman called— He is very pleasing, uniting the manners of a gentleman, with the simplicity & feelings of a boy—a most uncommon & agreeable mixture—and carries a letter of recommendation visibly written in his open countenance—which I trust will not be effaced by an abode in the seat of learning— <*One line washed out*> Mr & Mrs Hoffman sail for Europe on Wednesday—leaving their only son & daughter in Cambridge till they return!—

Friday 26th Mama & Sophia paid visits— In the eveg—Mama, Sophia & I went to the Theatre—Edmund & Mrs Parker with us— The play was Fasio, which I had seen before, but was even more struck by Miss Kembles wonderful powers, that at its first representation perhaps from knowing the story I was not as much interested, & therefore could attend more entirely to her astonishing force, grace & expression— Mr Kemble had injured himself by some accident, & was quite lame, which I regretted on Mama's account, as he is as graceful as his daughter.— The house was very full and fashionable—and all universally touched—or rather impressed—for there is nothing of the same kind of touching scenes as in "the Stranger."— It was astonishing "grand magnifique"—but did not go to the heart like Mrs Haller.— Came out to Cambridge by moonlight & passed an agreeable eveg.—

Saturday 27th Mama, Sophia & I went up to Mt. Auburn & passed the morning in wandering among the tombs. The place looked beautifully & is astonishingly improved. Mr Woolsey & Mr Felton called in our absence. In the afternoon Mary Jane & Josiah came— Had quite an agreeable visit—

Sunday 28th— Morng. Dr Ware— Messrs Bowen & Pritchard dined here— Two very pleasing young men, tho' they were frightened half out of their senses— Afternoon Mr H Ware—Edmund & Horace in the eveg.—

Monday 29th— Morning Mr Wm. Wells called very agreeable indeed.— Eveg. Sophia & I went to town—to a party at Mrs Crownin-shields[29]— House extremely elegant—the most so I think of any house in Boston— It was a supper party & every thing in the highest style—all the ladies & gentlemen very fashonable— Talked a long time to Tom Dwight, then to Mr Hooper—John Codman—Mr B. Crowninshield, with whom I went into the other room—there found Miss Kemble & her father— Miss K looked very well, not as handsome as I have seen her—elegantly dressed— She had just come from acting Mrs Beverly in the Gamester, & consequently some what fatigued— Mr Kemble I admire very much— he is, as the New Monthly says of him, "the perfect gentleman a character which he would find it difficult to divest himself of, either on or off the stage"[30] There is an affectionate affability and yet a perfect dignity in his manners united with ease & grace, which is very pleasing, & as rare as it is agreeable.

Went into Supper with Mr Crowninshield very superb— After supper talked to Mr Church, who was as silly as usual— then to Mr Chaplain, who seemed in such a bewildered state of mind, that I hardly knew what to make of it—but set it down as "another mystery"— Miss Goldsbor-ough sang—but does not sing with expression enough to give me any pleasure. The handsome Silsbee next approached, & we took two or three turns around the apartments, & soon after took leave— It was quite a pleasant eveg. Sophia went out of town, but I staid in as I wanted to go to the Fair Exhibition the next day.—

Tuesday 30th Called on Delia Gardner, at Mrs Minots— then went to Lucillas— Joined Louisa, & Delia, at Mrs. Millers, & proceeded to Faneuil Hall, to the Exhibition of the Fair articles—the sale being the next day[31]— On the way met Mrs T Coolidge & Miss Goldsborough—& the picked up Mr French Gray—Mr Bradbury, & Mr T Coolidge who went in with us—

The Hall looked very handsome, & decorated with Evergreens & flowers, & surrounded by the tables covered with every description of "articles"— Mrs. Otis was in her element—& Mr Church as one of her principal marshalls not less so— The other ladies I did not know except Mrs Everett. There were a great many people there, but not very crowded, so that we could really look at the tables— Leut Sawyer gave his arm & we promenaded the room some time—

Then Mr Robert Storer came up, & I gladly exchanged Mr Sawyer for Mr Storer—& with him took another tour— I believe you used to know & to like Mr Storer in former days, and if he was as pleasing then, as he is now I certainly agree with you— There is something so truly excellent & sensible in his appearance & conversation, & so gentlemanly in his manners that I was quite pleased— After we had taken several tours round the room, Louisa & Mr Sawyer, Mr Storer & myself, ajourned upstairs to the gallery where we commanded a perfect view of the whole scene, which was very pretty & animated.

Here we seated ourselves, & remained nearly an hour, conversing, & gasing on the changing scene below— We then returned to the lower floor, & again visited the different tables.— The gentlemen then walked home with us & truly Mr Storer had some what of a tramp of it from Faneuil Hall to 50 Chesnut St. The wind was a perfect gale, & the robes of the fair ones were elevated nearly to their heads. Mr Storer endeavoured to hold mine down, but we at last left them to their fate— Notwithstanding this little contretemps we had a very pleasant walk—Mr Storer being very agreeable.— So *real*— there are no "*mysteries*" about him certainly.— At the door we parted & I suppose the years of a residence in Boston will pass before Mr Robert Storer & I ever take another walk together—

After dinner took a nap, & after a short visit to Louisa, at Mr. H Hubbards, went to Mr Parkers, to accompany Lucilla & Edmund to the Theatre to see the Kembles in "Much ado about Nothing." Found E. Grant in the parlour—had a few strains of sentiment— After tea—Edmund, Lucilla, Miss Tidmarsh & myself walked to the Theatre. Arrived quite early— had quite a good box— Before the play began Mr Chaplain came round & favored me with a few words, tho' by the way he almost frightened me out of my wits. I had just seen him on the opposite side of the house, gasing in an a<page damaged>t manner thro' a box door—and before I could have thought it possible he could have turned round he spoke directly in my ear—causing me to jump in an unbecoming manner— "A horde of feirce barbarians" [32] soon after rushed into the next box, displacing Mr Chaplain, & leaving me to my meditations.—

I must refer you to the next volume for an account of the eveg— I did not know I was so near the end of this, or should have calculated better than to have broken off in the midst of an evening.—<*here ends volume 1*>

—Tuesday eveg—continued— The play now commenced—& we were extremely delighted with Mr Kembles Benedict—he was perfect— I cannot imagine anything better—such a perfectly gentlemanly, & characteristic performance, so delicate & yet so playful & spirited— The change from Benedict the determined bachelor—to "Benedict the married man" was admirable, sustained by every look & motion. Miss Kemble as Beatrice, was spirited but is affected I think in Comedy, which is certainly not her forte— She looked very handsome—most elegantly dressed.— There is a great deal that is very disagreeable in the play, but still I can never regret having seen the inimitable Benedict.—

Our comfort too, was somewhat disturbed by our next neighbours, the next box being partly filled by a party of half sort of gentlemen, who had been dining together, & who had apparently "passed the genial bowl", more freely, than soberly.— They were fortunately too much stupefied to be noisy but were very disagreeable. We staid to the after piece which was very good—"Raising the Wind" in which Barrett acted Jermey Diddler, extremely well.[33]— The Theatre however struck me this eveg as more disagreeable than in any of our late frequent visits to it— Something perhaps must be allowed for the impressions of our next neighbours—the less fashionable aspect of the audience, and the disagreeables of the scenes in parts of the play—but still, it is certainly, even at the best, no fit place for "*an elegant female*".—

CHAPTER 3

Manners and Mores of
Cambridge and Boston Society

May 1833

This month proved no exception to Anna Quincy's normally full social cal-
endar. She recorded only five days (4, 9, 14, 21, and 29 May) in the entire
month when "No one came""or she "stayed home." The Quincy home in
Cambridge hosted a steady stream of callers, varying from those attending
planned social events to informal, drop-in visitors. Most callers came in
the afternoon, or later for tea and an evening's visit, which sometimes included an impromptu concert. Formal affairs included cotillions, usually in
Boston, or events such as the Hill wedding reception. Two examples give
the range of visits and visitors to Wadsworth House: on 16 May in what
Anna calls a "social meeting," the Sparks party come in the early evening to
view illustrations from Audubon's *Birds of America*, are served tea, and stay
until 10 P.M. By contrast, on 8 May Anna spontaneously invites a riding
party to come in out of the rain.

According to Anna's diary, the Quincy women spent most of their time
during the day receiving visitors or paying calls, domestic life being almost
purely social. Even when the family stayed home by themselves, they
engaged in a popular custom of the day, reading aloud novels and other literary works. Apparently, Anna and her sisters performed very little house-
work; aside from visiting, their typical day consisted of trips to Boston or
other nearby towns, shopping, or visiting cultural attractions in the morning, followed by dinner at home around 1 P.M. Because of the custom that
young unmarried women should not venture out alone, walking parties
were organized to such sites as Mt. Auburn and the Botanical Garden in
Cambridge.[1] Some days, Anna went with her mother on country drives to
Mt. Auburn, Brookline, or Quincy.

For women of Anna's station, churchgoing often figured as a major social activity. Yet these services receive little attention in Anna's diary. In May
she accompanies her father to the college chapel on three Sundays, but on

two she stays home. The Quincy family, like most upper-class people in the Boston area, were Unitarians. Anna notes sermons by the college divinity professor Dr. Henry Ware or his son, also Henry, but, except for a brief response ("very interesting discourse," 5 May) does not describe them. Perhaps she gives little space in her diary to churchgoing because she perceives no social or humorous dimension to it.

No doubt Eliza Morton Quincy schooled her daughters in proper social conduct just as rigorously as she acquainted them with the poems of John Milton and William Cowper. Because of her mother's training and example, Anna likely had no need to read the etiquette books of the day. Still, the precepts laid out by writers such as Eliza Farrar (the same Mrs. Farrar who called on 27 May) and Lydia Sigourney were ones followed in the Quincy household. In *The Young Lady's Friend* Farrar describes the mother's presence as a "welcome regulator" amid a group of young people.[2]

Implicit in Anna's descriptions is the sense of decorum that Farrar and others described in their manuals. Social visits should follow a proper pattern. For example, students and friends such as William Chaplain and Dutton Russell who are departing for home or Europe pay formal "take leaves." Some professors may linger indefinitely, but the governor of Massachusetts confines his "agreeable visit" to half an hour (31 May). Anna, her sister Susan, and her mother make a formal call to the Boston residence of the Crowninshields, where, after several minutes of waiting, a servant informs the ladies that the family is "not at home" (28 May). According to Farrar, morning callers could expect to be refused, since they might be trespassing on the only free time of the family.[3]

Regarding servants, the Quincys maintained a hierarchy similar to that of other wealthy households. In Anna's diary, the servants in Cambridge (Miranda, Betsy, and John) emerge primarily to announce callers; Anna does not mention their other numerous chores. Major Horace Bacon drives the carriage, and he has to relinquish his plans to attend President Jackson's visit to Charlestown on 23 June in order to ferry the Cambridge ladies there. In her autobiographical sketch, Anna Waterston mentions the family's policy of riding in the carriage to church on Sundays, thus depriving the coachman of a day off, and she recalls that the family gave little thought to inconveniencing a servant.[4] Except for her description of the West Point graduate Francis Vinton's exclaiming that Major Bacon outranks him (21 March), Anna treats servants as accepted and necessary presences.

No servant, however, announces the unanticipated call of Frederic Hoffman on 25 May, a visit that appears to distress the young hostess. The out-of-town visitors, the German writer Therese Robinson, her children, and Mrs. Crafts, were clearly invited, as was Ann Hoffman. But Frederic's sudden appearance lends to the occasion a sense of jarring disorder, with its "variety of people," an event that becomes nevertheless "an amusing afternoon" in the diary.

Recognizing the conventions of the day, Anna often ignores these strictures and in her diary uses them as occasions for humor. For example, young women were cautioned not to spend any unnecessary time alone with callers.[5] Anna no doubt exaggerates her discomfort on 2 May, when she exclaims over the impropriety of seeing Professor Follen and Harvard Overseer Porter "alone!!" Likewise, custom discouraged any contact between the informally clad horseback riders sitting in the parlor of Wadsworth House and the Harvard entourage entering the house after a theological lecture on 8 May. But, as Anna describes the entourage's "irruption of black coats, that overcame them like a summer cloud," she turns the contrast into a witty commentary: "The Presidential Hall, must have presented somewhat of an animated scene to various lookers on— The collection of gentlemen entering the front gate & this party of equestrians making their escape from the private portal, with servants &c in attendance."

May 1833

Wednesday—1st of May. Soon after breakfast Mama, Susan, & Sophia came in to go to the Fair— They drove off, & I went to Lucilla's—and we proceeded together to Faneuil Hall.— The mob—for I can call it nothing else, at the door & on the stairs was really overwhelming—but once in it there was no alternative, and on, on forever and age!— But it was severe to the last degree, at lenght the solid body of mortals were safely landed at the head of the stairs but on entering the Hall—the crowd was so immense that "'twere vain to tell thee all we felt"— As to approaching the tables—that was indeed a wild flight of imagination and after having been beaten about, by the unkind buffetings of fate, in the shape of ladies & gentlemen, we cast up our eyes, & saw Mama & her party, safely established in the gallery, looking down with infinite composure upon the Blind victims of Charity—who were twirl'd & hurled hether & twether with out any regard to name or place—

Lucilla & I determined to endure it no longer, and have paid an additional dollar— Soon found ourselves lifted up above all the disquietudes of the world below— And a most amusing scene it was—the ever changing crowd—the various dresses and figures—the airs & graces of the sellers—the flowers the dolls, the gay colours—the bus of a thousand voices, the variety of faces, and all the continual movements of the crowd formed altogether a most entertaining scene. Added to all the rest were a dosen cages full of Canary birds, who joined their distracting notes to the general din—till I was ready à la Ellen Keating to shake my fist at them.[6] I did give a look at one little rascal who was perched directly below me, that might have struck terror into the nerves of a Canary bird, but far from having any effect, he screamed louder than ever, tho' I have since thought it might have been from fright.—

Mean while the plot thickened below—and "beaux & belles and maids & madams", were seen bobbing about in all directions, and truly it was not a little amusing to sit calmly upstairs & seen all ones friends buffeting about below. "How patiently we heard them groan how glad the case was not our own." Mrs. Otis' voice was heard above all the rest, talking, laughing & selling— Louisa & I could not help being struck with contrast of this scene, and the one we were in a year from that day—at the Natural Bridge in the very depths of the Country—surrounded by "Nature in all her magnificence", so solemn so sublime, so silent—and a year from that very hour in this scene of things, surrounded by this immense crowd, with every colour of the rainbow flowers & feathers, & fripperies of all starts, this hum of men & women and canary birds and all *made up's*— I think there could not be a stronger contrast but could not then stop to moralise— There was indeed one thing that was Striking in this scene, which was several of the little blind Children, who were with the ladies behind the tables—unable to see, how strangely all these sounds must have seemed to them— It was quite affecting to see these little creatures, and truly it seemed a benevolence most praiseworthy which endeavoured to throw some light upon the darkness that must ever surround them.

We remained in the gallery the rest of the morning, not many people came up there, but so much the better those who did. I wanted to purchase some flowers, & "searched carefully among the crowd" for "some man of sense"—some Mr Robert Storer, to beckon up, & send as my *almoner* to the tables— But alas! a man of sense is not so easily found— Mr Robert Storer never appeared, and had not Edmund came up, & brought with him two beautiful bunches of flowers one for Lucilla & one for me, I might have gone to the fair for nothing. We did not attempt to go again upon the floor—but passed a very amusing morning—

In the afternoon went up to see Martha— Interrupted a tête à tête for which I am sure she must have thanked me, for Mr Woolsey looked as if he had not spoken for the last hour.— He is a perfect stick, in my humble opinion & if he has agreeable qualities they are as "well concealed" as Hannah's beauty.— I talked to Martha, while Mr Woolsey sat by, listening to every word without speaking, which I consider as one of the most enviable sensations, I mean to the *unhappy talker*, who knows that every word is weighed—and alas, knows too well that many must be found wanting— At last I could endure it no longer—and fled upstairs to Mrs Salisbury, where Martha joined us— Mr Woolsey taking his departure, & there we enjoyed an hour of feminine *chit-chat*, unawed by the by the glassy eyes of the stiff Greek professor[7]—

One piece of news did indeed overwhelm me— The great Wigram estate is gone and forever— Young Mr Salisbury is engaged—and there is no hope, no chance left of my ever being at the head of the great Worcester estate, unless he should become in some future day a widower! Oh Miss Dean, your *living* may one day yet be mine— "tho' the best laid plans of mice and men", seem to be flustrated by your unexpectedly bold stroke for a fortune![8]— The *Clergy* seem to be my evil geniuses— I am doomed to be supplanted by a Dean, deserted by a Clark, bewildered by a Chaplain—and wearied by a Church— Tell me not that some *rich* hearts may yet remain— There may be *sermons* in *stones*, but theres no truth in Man— nor woman either. Tell me not that a glass of "Flip" may yet again sparkle before me— Has not that been offered to "forty six sweethearts" in every city north of the Potomac, and heaven knows how many south of it—till nothing is left but the froth at the top, and the dregs at the bottom—

I've tasted enough of that mixture to satisfy one of the "forty six" that theres precious little refreshment <*a page is cut out here, but there are no apparent omissions*> there— Do not even point to a Springfield Elm or a Cedar of Gardner— What are trees compared with Gold! No— Unless you can make over a good solid gold mine attempt not to console me—for nothing else, can equal the grandeur of being Countess of Salisbury & at the head of the great Worcester estate.— After my visit was over—Sophia & I returned to Cambridge.—

Thursday 2d— All went to town Save me— Dr Follen—& Dr Porter
came! how dangerous—I saw them alone!!— In the eveg—young
Hoffman—& his sister came— Two very pleasing young people— I do
not know when I have seen so much ease and good manners, at once so
unaffected & natural— They are to remain in Cambridge during the absence of their father & mother probably two or three years. Frederics
manners to his little sister are really charming

Friday 3d— Mr Chaplain called early—to pay his farewell visit— The
only unwelcome visit which Mr Chaplain ever paid— Farewell, is a black
word—and all the poets & poetesses in the world can't make it otherwise— A *last* meeting is always painful, & it would be affectation to deny
that we much regretted the last visit of Mr Chaplain— But we "must not
dwell on themes like this—" Mr Chaplain expressed—& seemed to feel,
much regret at taking leave—& when he left us, carried with him the best
wishes of his N. England friends.9— Mama & Susan paid visits &c the
morng.—

Saturday 4th Mama went to Dedham taking Mrs. Appleton with her.—
Sophia went to town with Papa, at the request of Mary Jane to pass a few
days.— We walked to the Botanic garden.10— Soon after our return received a letter from Mrs. Dr Channing—dated Dedham & saying that
Aunt Dowse had been quite ill & requesting one of us to come over & stay
a few days— As soon as Papa returned Susan decided to go—& after
"forcing down a couple of mouthfuls" they were off— I passed the afternoon in solitary magnificence.— Mama returned about 7—had left Aunt
much better—but was still very glad that Susan had gone.—

Sunday 5th Morng Papa & I represented family at the Chapel—Dr
Ware.— Mr Wells dined here—as agreeable as usual— Josiah also came
out after dinner.— Mr. Henry Ware preached in the P.M. a very interesting
discourse.11— Edmund came out to tea—& was I believe our only visitor.

Monday 6th Called on Abby Phillips who was not at home.— Soon
after my return Mr Dutton Russell was announced— He came to pay a
preparatory visit to his departure on a six months tour thro' Europe.— I
give all due credit to the desire he doubtless had to bid us adieu—to see
us before he sailed—& will only mention, en passant—that there was an
introductory letter to Lafayette which was desirable, & which Mr Quincy
was kind enough to provide him— On parting I begged Mr Russell not to
be too overpowering on his return, & told him that an unaffected travelled

gentleman would be a delightful novelty— He assured me that he fully intended to return as much of a Yankee as he went—& so we parted—& doubtless when we meet again he will be a finished man!— Mr Woodward next called.—

In the afternoon Mama & I took a drive—calling for little Miss Hoffman & taking her with us. We had a very pleasant one & brought her home to tea—at which her brother joined us.— Ann, is a little oddity, full of the life & spirits saying every thing that comes into her head—& as easy as possible—evidently a great pet—but not disagreeably spoiled. Young Hoffman is very pleasing & his manners to his little sister charming— We passed quite a pleasant eveng—as there is *certainly* no difficulty in entertaining them.—

Tuesday 7th Morning— Staid at home—drew & Mama read loud in Mansfield Park.[12] In the afternoon Mama & I went to town— I called to see Delia, & Mary, who are to depart for Gardner immediately— Then called on Lucilla—found her prepared for going to the Theatre. Mama soon called for me, & we returned home through Brookline. Had delightful drive—Country looking exquistely— Papa received yr. letter from Columbia, which greatly delighted him.— Eveng. read loud in Mansfield.—

Wednesday 8th. Morng. Mama went to town, & brought Sophia out— In the afternoon Mama & Sophia went to the Chapel, to attend the Dudlean lecture, preached by Mr Francis of Watertown.[13]— Soon after they were all housed a "confounded looking black cloud" was rising— I watched it from the window, & listened to the distant peal of the thunder—

After I had completed my toilette—I was gasing out of one of the side windows at the threatening clouds, from which a few drops began already to fall, when round the corner of the church comes, a riding party consisting of two ladies, & a gentlemen, full speed.— In common humanity—I determined to call them in—"Seeing that they were ladies and as such entitled to my respect." I had just commenced a screaming message to John when the front door flys open, & the gentleman appeared. I begged him to ask the ladies to alight, & sent John out to assist them— the rain just beginning to pour down—

In the ladies came, & proved to be Miss Carter & Miss Sigorney—who it appears sat out to pay us an afternoon visit & were caught in the shower— Having sent away the horses—& the gentleman being introduced as "Mr Lunt"—we all seated ourselves, to wait till the shower was over—

The first half hour did very well, but as I had the whole avalanche of Clergymen hanging over my head, I was rather desirous to see my fair equestrians off—

After a visit of about an hour—Something was said of departing, & as the rain was over I made no objection— Seeing at this moment an array of hats, over the fence, & knowing thereby that the lecture was over, I advised the ladies to allow me to have their steeds brought to the back door, to which they assented. Meanwhile the gentlemen began to enter & Mama & Sophia also appeared— Many looks of curiosity were levelled at the two damsels, whose sweeping habits, riding hats, & whips, seemed rather inappropriate to the Clerical party assembled—

Seeing a fresh importatio[n] entering, I carried the ladies into the opposite apartment and explained the meaning of this second irruption of black coats, that overcame them like a summer cloud.— At last their horses were seen being led out & we took a short cut, through the back entry, & kitchen to the side door, where after some delay the ladies were at last mounted— The Presidential Hall, must have presented somewhat of an animated scene to various lookers on— The collection of gentlemen entering the front gate & this party of equestrians making their escape from the private portal, with servants &c in attendance. At lenght the young ladies were fixed to their satisfaction—& cantered off.—

I then returned through the little room, to the drawing room, where I found a goodly number of people assembled. Talked first to Mr Palfrey— then to Mr May, with whom I conversed the remainer of their visit— From what I could gather the injudiciously sensible Mr Francis had as usual preached every body out of patience & all seemed somewhat hot & desperate— Some cool lemonade & refreshing coffee however, set it all right—and "Mr May of Mays the mildest", chirped up in an agreeable manner— The gentlemen remained about an hour & then departed—

Thursday 9th Read—drew &c—all the morng— Received a letter from Sophia Morton[14] announcing the sad intelligence of Charlottes death— What a conclusion to that marriage!—

Friday 10th Wrote to Sophia M— Mr Bartlett called— In the evening— Judge Barnes from Phila his daughter & another young lady—& his two sons came— Miss Barnes quite a pleasing girl, very much like Caroline Denning.—

Saturday 11th Mama & Sophia went to Dedham.— Papa dined in town & I therefore passed the day alone in my glory— Mama & Susan returned

before dark.— In the eveg. Mr Gardner Mr May, & Mr Dwight (the divinity
Student) came.— The gentlemen gave us some delightful music—several
of the trio's were remarkably fine—very much in the Germans' style—
There is certainly no music equal to the human voice *divine*—don't accuse
me of a pun.—

Sunday 12th Did not go to church all day— Edmund & Horace Cleveland drank tea here.— Mr Whiting our eveg visitor—

Monday 13th Morning— Mr Woolsey called to take leave— Evening
Susan & I went in to town to go to see Miss Kemble, in Julia—(The
Hunchback). Went first to Mrs Millers had an interview with Mrs Russell
& Louisa— Louisa was to have come out with us to pass a few days but
after a dire debate decided to defer it— Edmund joined us—and at 7—
proceeded to the Theatre—were in No 3—excellent box— House full but
very unfashionable—

The play entirely depends upon the performance of Julia—& she did it
admirably— She looked exceedingly handsome dressed as usual most
magnificently— Kemble had contrived to make himself look like a perfect
fright— He acted the part of Clifford—(Julia's lover)—and looked about
old enough to be her grandfather— He was most unbecomingly attired,
with long corkscrew ringlets hanging over his face— He has really nothing to say, in his part & I should hardly have known him— Smith, as
Hunchback did tolerably—but all the weight of the play, fell on Julia—
She acted admirably—the celebrated "do it" was pronounced in a voice
which almost made the audience start,[15] & the tone in which she uttered
the other celebrated sentence— "Clifford, why don't you speak to me",
was one of her finest expressions.—

With all this, she was very little applauded—and there was but one
round of applause given to her the whole evening— She seemed excessively exhausted before it was over, & I really felt provoked at the audience
for not exerting themselves more— As the curtain fell, I mentally took a
final adieu of the fair magician, who certainly has excercised some power
over our minds—& certainly during her performances, over our feelings— There is nothing in the world, more beautiful, more striking, that
such a gifted, graceful woman—yet while we feel proud of her powers—
we cannot but regret to see them only employed in *acting*. However—if
she is satisfied, we have no reason, to wish it other wise— So farewell—
Fanny Kemble I thank you for the pleasure—& the pain you have given
me— You will be long remembered—

"The impassioned changes of thy speaking face
Thy stately form, and high imperial grace
Thy arms impetuous tost, thy robes wide flow
And the dark tempest gathered on thy brow,
What time thy flashing eye, & lip of scorn
Down to the dust thy mimic foes have borne
Remorseful musings, sunk in deep dejection
The fixed and yearning looks of strong affection
The actioned turmoil of a bosom rending
When pity, love, and honour are contending;—
Who have beheld all this, I ween!
A lovely, grand, and wondrous sight have seen
x x x x—
"Thy graceful form still moves in nightly dreams
And what thou wert, to the wrapt sleeper seems
While feverish fancy oft doth fondly trace
Within her curtained couch thy wonderous face.
Yea—and to many a wight—bereft and lone
In musing hours tho' all to the unknown
Soothing his varied course of good—or ill—
With all thy potent charm thou actest still"

So ends the Kemble Chapter.—

We returned home from the Theatre—found Mama, had not been all alone as some little youth has dropt in during the evening.—

Tuesday 14— Received yrs & Abby's letters from Columbia—with the news of Mr Greenes illness— So "first we were sorry & then we were glad again" Rained all day— Read loud in Northanger Abbey.[16]—

Wednesday 15th Wrote &c &c Afternoon Mama & I called for Anne Hoffman & then drove to Mt Auburn— Had a delightful drive & walk there.— Eveng— Finished Northanger.—

Thursday 16th Morng—drew &c. Mr Church called having sat up his nest, or rather commenced his wanderings, by establishing himself in Cambridge— He paid me a long visit & was as odd as ever— It has always been my opinion that he was a little distracted.— Expected a social meeting for Mrs. Sparks'— Prepared therefore asual on such occasions. Mrs. Sparks, & her Father & Sister, (Mr & Miss Allen) came before dark—in order to see Audubon's great book. Mr. Allen is a pleasing old gentleman,

& his manners' to his daughters, & theirs to him, are exactly what we admire—so affectionate & confiding, & yet so respectful & tender.

Miss Allen is much younger than Mrs. Sparks resembles Miss Silliman
in manner & somewhat in appearance, is very unaffected, and easy—
Mrs. Sparks we admire.— She resembles Mrs. Theodore Sedgwick very
much, tho' not as much ~~a lady of~~ accustomed to society as Mrs. S. & consequently not such ease of manner, until you are acquainted with her—
She appears to have *real* refinement, and is entirely free from the sickly
affectation, that sometimes passes for that rare possession. Has much
taste, particularly for painting in which she excells herself, & seems to
understand the value of all tasteful articles, better than any one I have
seen for a long time— We employed all the fleeting shadows—or rather
lights that remained, after their arrival, in "Oh'ing, & Ah'ing" over
Audubon—which of course met its meed of praise.

Before tea, we were joined by Mr & Mrs Palfrey, Dr Beck, Mr. Sparks, &
Mr Felton & Mr Alvord the "*Semi*" law professor.[17]— The social cup was
then passed round, & we sipped & "chatted" for the next half hour— Mr
Alvord was formerly here, as a law student, but had entirely faded from
my recollection being only an excellent person, & one of the most prom-
ising young lawyers, was in all probability not worth recollecting. In appearance he resembles Mr Fessenden & Sam Walley, but appeareth to be a
sensible sort of a well meaning youth.—

After tea Mama, Mrs. Sparkes, Mrs. Palfrey & Susan, ajourned into the
little room, to examine some of the numerous odditis there in enclosed,
while Miss Allen & myself attended by Mr. Felton & Mr. Alvord, wandered
around the room to consider the various productions of the pencil, which
decorates it while the other gentlemen vibrated— Miss Allen, seemed to
know a good deal about pictures, but the two gentlemen both as blind as
beetles, could not have been much edified, as probably they hardly knew a
horse chesnut, from a Chesnut horse, on canvass.— Mr. Alvord indeed
was arrested by the picture of J. Quincy jr & made some appropriate *law*
salutation[18]—

When this survey was over, we gathered round the centre table &
books & prints & conversation enlightened us—inspirited by the heart-
stirring laugh of Mr Felton— The bugs & butterflies were also gallanted
on to the table & added to the general mellée of the eveg—which certainly
could not be called a stupid one, if locomotion is an ingredient in an animated one— For nobody sat still a moment but roved, as Mr. Vinton

would say—in "a butterfly state from flower to flower"—& from bird to bird, & book to book— The company remained until 10 o'ck—& I hope passed an agreeable evening— We certainly did—"and thats something".— A great fire was beheld just after their departure, which however—only proved to be a barn full of hay—but the light was very great—

Friday 17— dull day—drew—commenced my first drawing in water colours—note it down, so that if I ever become a great artist, this leaf may be placed in some great collection of valuable records!— To you, my dear Mrs Greene I dedicate it, as it was with the colours presented by you, this great genius, first flourished a brush.— F Hoffman called—as pleasing as ever

Saturday 18th Went into town, while Mama went on to Dedham. Called at Lucillas, & had a two hours gossip with her—heard descriptions of Miss Kembles last appearance &c—and also of the pamphlet entitled "Scenes at the fair"—imputed to Mr. Parish—very well done, but very impertinent.[19]— Dined with Lucilla, & passed the P.M. with [Martha]— Returned to Cambridge. Mr. Folsome in the eveg—

Sunday 19th Did not go to church in the morng— Mr Wells dined here.— Afternoon went to the Chapel. Mr Henry Ware—very interesting.— After tea Edmund came out— Read the letters loud to him &c— Horace Cleveland also came, & after their departure Messrs. Crafts & Ruteledge.— Youths rather hard to entertain— Rutledge looking as if he had not energy enough to open his mouth, & Crafts almost biting yr. head off, by his grumpy way of speaking, present somewhat of a singular contrast.—

Monday 20th Morning drew &c. Called to see Mrs Robinson, the german lady who is staying in Cambridge— Afternoon, Henry Cleveland called— Should hardly have known him "quite a dandy"— Hat in hand, frockcoat on back, and whiskered cheek—quite a foreign tournure, & vastly improved. Conversed upon the usual *return* topics, hopes & fears, pleasures, expectations & solicitudes, anticipations, retrospections & reflections in general. Could hardly believe that it was 3 years since that Sunday morning Horace & he took leave in Chesnut St— Can't you see them now shackling out of the parlour door— Est il possible?— Mr Cleveland paid an agreeable visit, & when he took leave, did *not shackle* out of the apartment.—

Tuesday 21st Rainy disagreeable day—drew—& read old journals till we were nearly *frantic*. I believe no=body came—

Wednesday 22d A most delicious day— Mama & I drove over to Brookline, never saw any thing to equal the beauty of the country—the clouds & the flowers, & the trees & the meadows & the birds & the brooks—one continual garden— Arrived at Mrs. Russells. Saw the ladies—seemed rather out of spirits— Louisa looked pretty however— Decided to come to Cambridge on Friday. After paying a reasonable vis took leave, & drove into town— Went to Whitakers where Mama & I had much amusement, & then drove out of town.

Reached home to a late dinner—had a delightful morning.— Found we had lost visits from Mrs. Sparks, Miss Allen, & Mr Bennett Forbes.— Afternoon Mr & Mrs. T. Coolidge & Miss Goldsborough— The two ladies not withstanding the negligence of their attire, very pleasing, there is something loveable about them— Discussed all manner of things with Miss Goldsborough, South, North, east, west,— & had quite a pleasant visit from them.— After their departure Mr. & Mrs. Craft,—one of the innumerable little crafts came.[20]—

Thursday 23d— Morning drew—&c. Afternoon Mrs. Allston came. Then yr. & Abby's letter from Charlotte came in—with the account of yr. departure from Columbia, & I assure you we felt quite sorry to leave that agreeable City, forever—altho' we have only a paper acquaintance with it.— After reading the letter, we drove to Mt Auburn which never looked more lovely. Wandered about for a long time— Perfectly delightful. —

Friday 24 Fine day— Mama & Susan, taking Mrs. Robinson with them went to town— Sophia & I walked to the Botanic Garden— Weather perfection, country looking delightfully— Mr Carter very polite gave us flowers & furnished us with chairs, & we sat under the trees for a long time. Soon after our return visitors were announced, & I desended.— Found two ladies—a fat gentleman & a little girl— One lady advanced in a most friendly manner, pronouncing the name of *Mrs. Hodges*, introduced the other lady as "my Sister," & the gentleman as Mr. Hodges.

Who they were was passed my comprehension, but as they appeared to know every member of our family, together with all our relations, plans, life, & circumstances in general, I thought it would be unpardonable in me, not to know them, so I endeavored to throw all bewilderment from my manner, what ever was the State of my mind. We conversed upon various topics—and at last Mrs Hodges, after asking some questions about the family pictures, said she felt interested in them as she was a desendant of Edmund Quincy's![21]— This capt the climax & who they could be,

Afternoon went to the Chapel. Mr Henry Ware — very interesting. — After tea Edward came out — Read the letters loud to him &c. Horace Cleveland also came, & after their departure [...] Crafts & Rutledge. — [...] rather hard to entertain — Rutledge looking as if he had not energy enough to open his mouth, & Crafts almost biting up head off, by his grumpy way of speaking, [...] somewhat of a singular Contrast. —

Monday 20th Morning drew &. Called to See Mrs Robinson, the german lady who is staying in Cambridge —

Afternoon, Henry Cleveland called — Should hardly have known him 'quite a dandy' — Hat in hand, frock coat on back, and whiskered cheek. — quite a foreign tournure, & vastly improved. Conversed upon the usual return topics, hopes & fears, pleasures, expectations & solicitudes, anticipations, retrospections & reflections in general —

Diary entries for 19–20 May 1833.

grew every moment more pussling— At last upon her saying something about her Mother—it flashed into my mind, that it might be Miss Dolanson, who as I had never seen, & Mrs Hodges I had never even heard of, it was not surprising that I should not know them. They proved to be the very same, however, & I made this discovery just as they were taking leave, but I do not think they perceived that I did not know them.— They were quite pleasing, & I was sorry I had not been better enlightened before their departure.

Mama & Susan returned to dinner after passing an agreeable morning. Brought word that Louisa was too much indisposed to come this afternoon to begin her visit as was arranged. In the afternoon Mrs Grant & Elisabeth came— E. looked very pretty indeed— Had quite a pleasant visit from them.—

Saturday 25th Morning— Sophia & I walked. Mama & Susan visited—

Afternoon— Sent the carriage at 5 o'clk for Mrs. Robinson, who accordingly arrived followed by her german servant, the baby, & her little girl— The carriage was then dispatched for Mrs. Crafts who was also to drink tea here. We then roved round the rooms, playing with the baby, who is the drollest little thing only three months old, very intelligent with immense blue eyes, and arrayed in a long white frock, with very large *bishop sleeves*, buttoned round its wrists. The little girl is the image of Susan Clarke, & chatters German & English as fast as possible, altho she is only three years old.— Mrs. Crafts now enters, & is ushered into the apposite room, where the carpet was down, where Mama & Sophia joined her—I resigning the baby to Mama, for the dear little thing almost broke my arm off it was so heavy & returned to Susan & Mrs. Robinson, who were looking at the cherubs.

Just then the door opens & in walks Frederic Hoffman— I knowing that Mama expected his sister, presumed of course he had been invited also, & immediately inquired whether Ann was not with him— He looked rather bewildered, & replied ah no—he had not seen her that day—merely called himself "having half an hours leisure." At this moment the little Robinson flies in to the room bearing in her arms the doll Charlie, & commences an animated—address in *german* to her mother. Hoffman turned with an bewildered air, to gase upon this little oddity chattering in this unknown tongue and had a vista thro the open doors of Mama & Mrs. Crafts on a distant Sopha, Mama holding in her arms the Bishop sleeved Baby—

At the same moment the front door flies open & two forms enter, Sophia is seen moving swiftly along, & on meeting one, which I knew to be Elisa Guild a *salute* is seen between them, while the other who proves to be Ann Hoffman, flies into the room where we were sitting— Hoffman seemed completely bewildered at the babel of *tongues*, & the variety of people, & the sight of his sister who he had no idea was coming, for, as I afterwards discovered, his visit was entirely accidental—

However we soon collected our scattered ideas, tho' our attention was somewhat distracted.— Elisa only staid a few moments & then vanished— Frederic Hoffman, only remained until the prayer bell rang—& soon after the children being sent home, some order was restored— Dr Beck joined us at tea—& after that I entertained Ann Hoffman, who is very odd, & very much of a spoiled child. I thereby lost much amusing conversation between Mrs. Robinson Dr Beck & the rest of the party. Nor can I give any idea of half the absurdities that took place.— F Hoffman returned in the course of the eveg for his sister—& is a very pleasing young man.— About 9 o'ck—the Carriage was ordered & our visitors transported home, after certainly affording us an amusing afternoon.—

Sunday 26th Rainy day, did not go to church.— Edmund came out to tea— In the evening, Mr Dabney, & Mr. Alvord called.—

Monday 27th— Morning— Drew &c— Mrs. Robinson & Mrs. Farrar & Mr. Clarke the divinity student called — Afternoon Sophia & I walked Mary Jane & Josiah came out—drank tea here.—

Tuesday 28th Morning— Mama, Susan & I went into town, drove first to the Athenaeum— Not many people there. Pictures beautiful— Some of the old masters, such as never visited my dim eyes before.[22] Also a wonderful drinking cup, carved by some Artist, hundreds of years ago—representing the Greeks & Turks at war— Little Mr. Eliott, attended me about to view the wonders of nature & art, while Susan & Mama wandered at a distance. There were not the usual assortment of odiosities, staring from the Sophas—which rendered it most agreeable.— After we left the Atheneum went to some Shops— In Mrs. Gregorys encountered Mrs. Harry Otis—who arrayed in a most fantastic manner flew upon me, with open arms, & commenced the usual flow of conversation. Thanks for the portfolios I made for her table—&c—then an account of a visit she received last eveg from Lawrie Todd—&c— Kept me at least a quarter of an hour, and entertained the usual collection of girls & women, at Mrs Gregorys until I at lenght broke away in the middle of her story.—

Joined Susan at Mrs. Millers, & made various visits. No one visible—
Were admitted at Mrs. Crowninshields shown thro' a suite of splendid
apartments, & allowcd to mediate on their varied beauties until the servant ascertained that the ladies were not at home. Returned to Mrs.
Millers, & joined Mama—desended & were assisted into the carriage by
John Codman who *actually* looked handsome!!— Then drove to Cambridge.—

Afternoon was just enjoying a sweet oblivious antidote to the fatigues
of the morning, when Miranda knocked at the door, with Abbys letter
from Lunchburg— Started up & read it with great pleasure—quite as refreshing as a nap would have been— Shall be glad however when you are
all safe at home, tho' we shall miss the agreeable letters sadly.— In the
evening went to a fête at Mrs. Becks—for Mrs Robinson— Had a decent
sort of a time. Talked a long time to Edward Channing—& then to Mr Felton, who was remarkably agreeable. Not much room however for description.—

Wednesday 29th Mama & Susan went to Boston, Brookline & Dedham.
Sophia & I remained at home. I drew & Sophia read loud in that most
profitable volume—an old journal!— No one I believe broke in upon our
solitude.— Mama returned about 9 o'clk. having left Susan at Mrs.
Guilds

Thursday 30th Mary Jane & the bablings dined here—quite an agreable
day— Mrs. Parker & Lucilla called in the afternoon— In the evening
Mama Sophia & I accompanied by Mrs. Robinson went to a party at Mrs.
Parks.[23]— An assemblage of most of the Cambridge worthies—Mr. Osgood (the Divinity Student) armed me down in to the parlour, & conversed for some time. Is not particularly pleasing, being more desirous of
using the eloquence of his fine eyes, than in being otherwise entertaining. Then talked to Mrs. Crafts, who dilated upon "the varied absurdities"
of "George & Mr Gray," & particularly that of their utterly refusing to accompany her to the party. Edward Channing then joined me, & we had a
long confab. he being to me of the most truly diverting peices of disagree-
ableness in Cambridge. Among other things we discoursed upon dress,
rouge & fashion—& the various methods of making *gentlemen's* lower garments!— A long talk with a Miss Gorham, an everlasting [proser]—but
with the remains of great beauty—& closed the performances, by a few
words with Mr Folsom.—

Sophia in the meantime was *flirting* in the perspective with Mr Red-haired Fuller, & Mr. Newell the PostMaster. From such "gallant gays"[24]—however, we summoned her. On going to the carriage Mrs. Robinson preceeded me, leaning on the *arm* of Mr Peabody—who *gracefully* bowing at the carriage door, to those within, made a most unfortunate attack upon the fragile forms of Mr. Folsom & me, & were bringing up the *rear*.— However we were fortunately not annihilated—but proceeded homewards— Not a word was exchanged about the eveg but in the course of the drive Mrs. Robinson spoke of the balls she had been in the habit of attending in St Petersburg!—

On our return home found Papa in the parlour & just returned from the feild of battle, between the collegians & the workmen who were raising the church, who had been having "a smart *fit*" as Larry would say, but who were separated by the force of the Presidents arm.[25]— The unlucky Ruteledge, received a rap over the head, from one of the men, which has been the most serious consequence of the affray, but which we hope will not be materially so to him—

Friday 31st— Delightful day— In the morng Mama Sophia & I drove to Quincy—had a delightful drive. Country looking beautiful— Quincy looked delightful & the place very good order. Staid there a long time wandering about, & sitting on the porch— Then returned through Boston, to Cambridge to dinner— Had a delightful morning.—

In the afternoon had just arose & put on my clothes after a refreshing nap, when Miss Robbins is announced & immediately after Mr Grenville Mellen entered. Mama was summoned, & agreeable converse ensued— but they did not remain long— Dr Bancroft next entered on the scene, & remained so long that we began to fear the good man never intended to depart. Mrs. Minot was next announced & I joined the groupe— Mrs. M was quite agreeable brought a letter from Mary— Mr. Henry Ware then entered & tarried a few moments— Dr Bancroft, staid to tea, is quite my beau ideal of a old man, with out any of the disagreeables of one.

After tea Papa accompanied him to Divinity Hall, & just after their excit the strait figure of his excellency Govr. Lincoln appeared— He paid us an agreeable visit conversing on various interesting topics for half an hour. Notwithstanding his formality, his gentlemanly manners are very pleasing, & I for one of his subjects regret that his reign is nearly over.— Evening roved about the rooms & talked by moonlight.—

CHAPTER 4

President Andrew Jackson Visits Harvard

June 1833

In her diary entry for 24 June, Anna facetiously terms the vacillating social arrangements for President Andrew Jackson's visit to Cambridge as a "catastroph." Yet truly controversial, if not quite catastrophic, was Harvard University's decision to confer an honorary degree on the seventh U.S. president (1767–1845) when he visited the Boston area.

The controversy stemmed from several overlapping causes. First, most of Boston and Cambridge had been staunchly Federalist during the first decades of the nineteenth century. Anna's father had represented his district as a Federalist in Congress from 1805 to 1813, supporting a strong central government and distrusting a purely democratic one. The region had proudly supported Massachusetts native John Quincy Adams for president in 1824 and again in 1828. In both those elections Adams had been opposed by Andrew Jackson, a general who became a popular hero after leading the U.S. Army to victory over the British in the 1815 Battle of New Orleans. In the 1828 presidential election Jackson had prevailed, making Adams the only one-term president to date besides his father, John Adams.

In his diary, John Quincy Adams's son Charles Francis Adams summed up the resentment against Jackson, shared by many in Massachusetts: Jackson "has served his Country no more usefully than a thousand others, but he has the prestige of military glory which dazzles all mortal minds. The art of killing is prized higher than the art of vivifying. My father who was his competitor for the Presidency and a man of incomparably superior character, yet carries with him perpetually a load of unpopularity."[1]

Jackson's image also provoked another cause of the controversy, since he represented a type of leader dramatically different from the aristocratic, intellectual New Englanders. He had fought Indians as well as the British; he came from a western state, Tennessee, and in his political campaign had championed the kind of backwoods frontiersman, an effective strategy for decades to come. Should this rough-hewn man, with little formal education, receive an honorary degree from the foremost educational institution in the United States? Former president John Quincy Adams refused to attend the ceremonies at his alma mater, stating in his diary of 18 June that he could not "witness [Harvard's] disgrace in conferring her highest Literary honours upon a barbarian, who could not write a sentence of Grammar, and could hardly spell his own name."[2]

Despite this opposition, Josiah Quincy and Harvard University took the unpopular step of inviting President Jackson to visit the school as he made his way through the northeastern United States in the spring and summer of 1833. On 13 June the Corporation agreed to confer an honorary LL.D. on Jackson, a decision ratified by the Board of Overseers on 22 June. Harvard thus continued its tradition of awarding this degree to any U.S. president (already received by George Washington, John Adams, Thomas Jefferson, James Monroe, and John Quincy Adams) visiting the university. On Saturday, 22 June, Massachusetts gave Jackson full honors, and "an immense number of his fellow citizens" came out to applaud the president as he paraded from his quarters in Tremont House to the State House. Later that afternoon at a ceremony attended by Anna's sister Susan and their mother on Boston Common, Jackson reviewed troops who "repeatedly and warmly cheered the President."[3]

Most of the planned activities honoring Jackson, however, had to be postponed. The president suffered a "serious indisposition," reported the *Boston Evening Transcript* on Monday, 24 June. This delay precipitated Anna's comment on that day, "All up in the wind again— All preparations thrown away," just as the Quincys planned a presidential reception at Wadsworth House. By Wednesday, 26 June, however, the president had recovered sufficiently to visit Harvard, and Anna awoke that morning to hear "Papa" exclaiming that Jackson would be in Cambridge at 10 A.M. Soon students and officials, along with Cambridge townspeople, gathered in the university's chapel to honor the president. Josiah Quincy addressed Jackson ("in English," the *Boston Courier* pointedly noted), proclaiming the achievements of Harvard and its hallowed history. Quincy added, "It is auspicious to the cause of science, when men in elevated stations, or those who are eminent for talents, or virtue, or influence, condescend to evince an interest in the seats of learning." President Jackson then "returned a short reply," after which he was addressed in Latin by a member of the senior class and awarded his honorary degree. According to Edmund, Jackson "submitted graciously to the Latin, bowed generally in the proper places, and received his parchment in eloquent silence, which was broken by general applause."[4]

Although Anna had elected not to attend the ceremony in the chapel, she later reported that it had proceeded "all in the happiest manner." Carefully attired, she awaited the president at Wadsworth House, where the rooms had been expeditiously set up for the reception. Harvard students escorted Jackson first to the library and then to the Quincy home, "where he was introduced to the Students and Faculty of the University."[5] Anna deemed him a "very gentlemanly old man," although quite frail.

The president's condition did not prevent a visit to the Bunker Hill monument in Charlestown, where he "ascended to the top of the unfinished monument, accompanied by the Vice President, Secretaries, &c, and remained some minutes evidently delighted with the surrounding prospect." After a tour of the Charlestown navy yard, he and his party left the city.[6]

The presidential thus visit passed without incident. Yet members of the Boston and Harvard community continued to criticize Josiah Quincy and university officials for their decision to award the honorary degree. The complaints continued through several university meetings before Quincy succeeded in convincing his critics that the degree had been appropriate.[7]

Unaffected by this controversy among New Englanders, Anna filled her diary with a lighthearted perspective on President Jackson's visit to Cambridge. Only the social activities paralleling his appearance commanded her attention. Receiving President Jackson in her home filled just a small part of the 26 June entry, a day that also included a trip to the Charlestown navy yard and a concert at the Masonic Temple in Boston. Of the presidential ceremonies at Harvard, Anna wrote, "all went off exceedingly well—have not time to do justice to half the absurdities of the morning."

June 1833

Saturday 1st of June. Morning Sophia & I went to town— After going to various shops, called on Elisabeth Grant & sentimentalised for some time—walked with Martha & c.— Very warm, & thankful to return to our cottage again.— Afternoon Mama took Mrs. Robinson to ride. The baby staid with us—a dear little thing. Mrs. R returned to tea & passed the eveg here— Is a very sensible lady, but speaks english so imperfectly as to render her conversation less agreeable than it would otherwise be.—

Sunday 2d Did not go to church in the morning. In the afternoon Josiah came out— all went to church—Mr H Ware—very interesting— Horace Cleveland walked home with us, drank tea here— Edmund came in just after—read Abbys letter &c &c. In the evening, came Judge Story Edward Chaplain, Mr Felton Henry Cleveland & young Mr King.— Talked most of the evening to Edward Chaplain, who is an interesting youth of eighteen summers— Very different

style from his brother, inferior in beauty, but otherwise quite his equal I
should imagine— Heard of our elegant friend's safe arrival in his native
woods wasting his *sweetness* on the desert air.[8]— Judge Story talked
asusal, but did not hear much that he said. Mr. Felton looked like a fright
but was quite agreeable. Henry the travelled Henry was at the other ex-
tremity of the apartment, & I did not even hear the sound of his voice.
Passed quite an agreeable eveg.—

Monday 3d Delightful Day.— Morning received yr. letter on the road to
Charlottesville and also one from Mary Minot at Gardiner. Mama &
Sophia paid visits all the morning.— In the afternoon called for Mrs.
Crafts, & took her to Mt Auburn. Walked in Mt A. in the afternoon looked
delightfully— It is really "as beautiful as a dream," as Mr. Willis would
say.— In the eveg—Mr. D. Davis came. Poor old man, it is indeed painful
to see him. He has almost entirely lost his mind, & is scarsely able to
make himself intelligable

Tuesday 4th fine day.— Morning went to town to spend a day or two
with Martha Salisbury. Passed the day with Mrs. Salisbury & M. in talking
&c &c. Eveg. walked in the mall. A Mr. Cutler drank tea at Mrs. S.—
Handsome, but excessively unpleasant.—

Wednesday 5th—Martha & I walked in the morng. & then sat in Mrs.
S's room & talked— Miss Tappan called, quite an amusing little body—
Passed the rest of the day talking &c—

Thursday 6th Martha & I walked—and then sat to gather until 12
o'ck—when the carriage came for me—took an affectionate adieu, after a
quiet but pleasant visit to them— Brought Cousin Nancy Tracy out of
town who was to pass a few days with us—found Elisa Guild, & all the
rest of the family in the parlour— Nothing very remarkable had occur'd
in my absence— In the P.M. Mr. Bromfield came.— Henry Cleveland
came in the eveg—did not see him however.—

Friday 7th Walked in the Morng— Mama & all save Sophia & I went to
town— Ann Hoffman came— Our interesting young friend Frederic,
Hoffman, has been attacked by a complaint of the lungs, & is quite ill—
We all feel as if it was one of our own family—& indeed the idea of such a
young man being arrested at the very beginning of his carreer, which
promised to be so bright & so successful, is really dreadful— But we hope
for the best—and trust that by care, & prudence he may yet to spared—
Ann appeared very cheerful, & remarkably pleasing. In the afternoon,
Mrs. Miller, Mary Jane & Josiah & Josy came out— All went up to Mt

Auburn— Ann Hoffman came in again & drank tea with us seemed— cheerful—& pleasing.—

Saturday—8th Mama, Mrs. Tracy, Elisa & I went to Dedham— I intended to have stopt at Mrs Russells, but hearing from Josiah that John Gore had just arrived thot it better to differ my visit— We had quite an agreeable ride, although the little carriage nearly shook us to pieces, & we all talked together & repeated poetry at the pitch of our lungs— Arrived at Dedham, & found Aunt Dowse quite ill, so much so as to be unable to descend— Cousin Nancy Storer however there & seemed very well— Dr Stimpson dined there which was at first thought rather malàprops as we wanted to have a holding forth together but it was not of [any] matter— Before we rose from table Mr. John Bromfield joined the motely group— But I was so weary with the riding & the talking that I soon sunk to my slumbers.—

We then visited Aunt Dowse—& at ½ past 4 again ascended the carriage & drove to Mrs. Guilds—had a delightful drive— Found Mrs. Guild at home & the place looking most beautiful. Walked about with the children who are dear little things.— Drank tea with Mrs. Guild, & then returned to Cambridge. Had a very pleasant ride— At home found yr. letter from the Natural Bridge, which we read with great satisfaction—am delighted to find that you were not disappointed—and anticipate much pleasure in comparing notes about it. Mama & Papa went down to Mrs. Curtis' to see about Frederic—who is still very sick—

—Sunday 9th— Morning—wrote &c. Edmund, Mr. Wells & Tom Davis dined here, had a very pleasant dinner— Afternoon read yr. letter to Edmund. Mrs. Tracy went to Waltham to pass the night— Josiah came out to tea— Read yr. letter to him, being the *fourth* time of reading.— Josiah & Tom returned after tea.— Evening Judge & Mrs. Story came & James Colman. James brought me an exquiste drawing for my book— Passed a very agreeable day all together— Excepting our anxiety about Frederic Hoffman—who was quite ill again that day—but Dr Warren gives it as his opinion that no immediate danger is to be apprehended.—

Monday 10th Morning—went in to town with Mrs Tracy & Elisa & Sophia, intending to leave them at the Atheneum & go out to see Louisa— Drove round to various places & at last stopt at Josiahs office, where we discovered that we had the lame horse in the carriage, so I was obliged again to give up my visit— After some debate we journied on towards the

Athenaeum— On the way Horace spied Mrs. Russells coachman in the street, he is accordingly hailed, & detained while I wrote a hurried scrip. to Louisa on a card telling her of my intended visit. Just at this moment up starts Papa from some neighbouring alley & joins the melay— He provided me with a piece of blotting paper as an envelope for my elegant note, the tout ensemble of which was touched up, by a piece of *twine* bound around it— We then sped away to the gallery, where we passed some time very agreeably— then called on Lucilla—& then came out of town.—

After relating our various experiences, & dining we had just sunk to our slumbers, when Mrs. Higginson sends word she will call for Elisa G. in three minutes, to take her to Brookline. The hapless Elisa was assisted in her toilette by Sophia & myself, arrayed fantastically in dressing gowns—& in that trim was very nearly caught by the travelled Henry, who was seen entering the drawing room, as we flitted across the top of the Staircase— He probably would have taken us for some Grecian Statues suddenly endowed with life[9]—which perchance had *followed him* from Italy.—

Elisa soon departed, & I after finishing my toilette, wrote a sentimental effusion to Julius Tower, who had called several times without seeing us—to ask him to come in the evening— I had just despatched it, & was almost regretting I had done so, as it was raining very fast, when a ring at the door attracted me to the Window, & I beheld to my astonishment, Louisa Gore, desending from a carryall—assisted by a frockcoated figure, which the eye of friendship recognised as the graceful John— Louisa, alone entered however, & was greeted with much surprise, as well as pleasure as the idea of her being well enough to venture out such a day quite petrified us.— Mr. John Bromfield, who I forgot to say was vibrating also, looked astonished on, at the kissings & exclaimings, & soon gathered up his mantle blue—& rushed from the apartment.— Louisa looked as if she had been sick, as well she may—as the poor child has really had a time of it—

We passed an hour talking & laughing very pleasantly, when, in the midst of a pouring rain, Mrs. Russell & John Gore are seen on the full run, entering the gate— Great was the rushing & the brushing & the shaking, & the oh'ing & the ah'ing—& at last all were comfortably settled. They had come from Mrs. Ingolsons, had been caught in the shower, taken refuge in Mrs. Newells porch until Mr. Church happened to pass with an umbrella which Mrs. Russell caught out of his hand, & leaving him perfectly bewildered as to where she was going, or where she had come from—rushed on to our house.—

John Gore—now I look at him with my glass—has somewhat improved since last we met—grown thinner & does not bark quite as much à la Crafts—as was his wont, "when he sailed, when he sailed"— Save this he seems the same, but has behaved with much forbearance towards his Mother & Mr Russell since his return, which is certainly more than could be expected. They remained about ½ hour—conversing agreeably & then all departed, in the same war of elements.—

After their departure discussed their merits & various other subjects, until about 8 o'clk, when I heard the steps of a carriage being let down at our door—well thinks I, here comes Julius, à la Leut. Porter.— In a few moments the door opens, & Julius enters—followed to our surprise by a female form in a bonnet & long white viel— What relation she held to friend Julius we were entirely at a stand to imagine but caught the name of Tower—and to our utter astonishment, upon a more minute enquiry, discovered that it was his wife!!¹⁰ Mrs Julius Tower!! We were guilty of the rudeness of starting as we had never even heard a whisper of a preparatory engagement—& here we were plunged at once into matrimony! With well recollected dignity however, Mama & I, covered our astonishment, but Susan did not recovered the shock for some time—

Julius sat down by Mama while I attacked Mrs Tower. She was not pretty, but had gentle & rather pleasing manners & seemed perfectly self possessed, altho' it was rather an embarressing situation, to be brought among strangers who she had never seen, & who had been unable to disguise their utter astonishment that such a person as herself was in existance— At first we were rather ashore for subjects, & having sung the praises of Charlemange, & Trenton falls, where at a stand, for Susan who was sitting by, gave me no sort of assistance.— However we made out pretty well, for half an hour, & then Julius made her change seats with him, & talked to us.—

He is the same excellent person, we formerly knew, & neither time, nor the cares of matrimony had wrinkled his calm brow, which bears some resemblance to that of the unparelled Charlemange. He seemed to be delighted to be again in Cambridge, & indeed we might have saluted him with the Eastern salutation—"felicity is painted on your countenance", for he really seemed to be perfectly happy, & as we find he has been married 8 months, we hope that Mrs. Tower has proved all his fancy painted her. We conversed on past times & future prospects very agreeably—& particularly about the flower—as well as the *Tower* of all our Cambridge acquaintance his interesting brother—

Indeed Charlemagnes praises were sounded from every side, & when Papa came down, & after all the introductions & greetings between him & Mrs. Tower were over—*he* took up the strain, & topt off all we had left unsaid. They staid until 10 o'clk & we had a very pleasant visit from them, & were much pleased by Julius, bringing his wife here without invitation showing as it did, that he believed—that the interest we always expressed towards him was sincere, & that it would also be extended towards her.— Adieus & messages were exchanged & they departed concluding the dramatis personae of this day—

After they were gone we again let loose our astonishment at this step of Julius, & much were they all amused at the idea of my writing a sentimental note to a young gentleman, as I thought, inviting him for the eveg. & then beholding him attended by a wife— Had it been the crown of Charlemange that was thus shared, *there* would indeed have been a fall, my, countrymen—but as only the Tower of Julius is taken we are entirely resigned.—

Tuesday 11th — Went into town quite early with Cousin Nancy— Went to the Athenaeum staid there until ½ past 11—& then called to see Martha—paid her a short vis & then joined Mama & Sophia in Chesnut St. & came out of town—leaving Cousin Nancy who was to go to Brookline to pass the night. Called at Mrs. Becks as we came out— Saw Mrs Hunt & Abby.—

Afternoon received yr. letter, written on board the steam boat describing the cave— You really seem determined to get your *joltings* worth—& have literally been above, about, and underneath,—& I expect that by the time you are forty you will, like Frederic, in the eléve of sensibility—tho' not I hope on so bootless an errand, "have proceeded during an unremitted space of many years, thro' Norway, Sweden, Germany, Holland, Italy, France, Spain, Portugal and the two Turkeys—& renewing your indefatigable perigrinations through Arabia, Asssyria & Egypt & following the course of the Nile, penetrate into the central regions of Africa, & thence, right onward, till you are unexpectedly bounded by the sea at the Cape of Good Hope," & I hope at last the mysterious "nods of a manderin of the Court of China," will give you a faint glimmering of the propriety of spending the rest of your days in New England.— We shall indeed be glad to see you again after this three months absence, & are indeed glad that you are alive to tell the story.— Mrs. Chaning & Mrs Dr Higginson called.—

Wednesday 12th Morning Mama went over to Brookline to bring Mrs Tracy back again— drew &c no one came— Mama & Cousin Nancy returned to dinner. Elisa Guild was to come back in the P.M. in order to go with Mama to the Hill nuptials, which were to be celebrated this eveg.— After dinner, e'er the Sleepers were aroused Mr John Bromfield arrived & staid some time. About six Elisa came in, bringing Mrs. Guilds dress who was to come & dress here for the wedding visit— Just as we had concluded tea, Edward Peirson, was announced, & summoned to join the social board. Every one however had finished, and as it was time for those who were to be present at "the joining of hands" to dress all vanished leaving Sophia tête à tête with the gallant Edward. Papa, Mama, & Elisa were bidden to the wedding while we humbler mortals were to come afterwards.

After they had departed, looking very well, Sophia & I commenced our toilettes—which concluded, we desended to the parlour where Edward Peirson like a second *Maitland*,[11] stood before the fire place to observe & moralise upon our gay dresses.— We waited a few moments for Mrs. Guild but as she did not arrive, took leave of Cousin Nancy, & Mr. Peirson, & drove to the Bridal: The house was quite illuminated & when we descended, we beheld already assembled, various worthies.— Mr [Pinter] Rodgers armed Sophia, while I *swept* up the glittering—ring with—Mr Johnson! Mrs. Phillips, & the three Miss Hills—looked uncommonly well being arrayed with much propriety & simplicity, with none of those questionable articles of dress, which they usually heap upon their persons.— After giving a congratulary *shake* to the Bride, I fell back—& being joined by Mr. Bassett had an agreeable talk— He looked extremely handsome & was very agreeable. Introduced Mr. Harry Tudor to me—& then we went into the other room—before which however I had a Grandison bow[12] from Dr Randall, who after asking permission to enquire after my health, with a medical look he proceeded to ascertain the state of mind & body of all my friends & relatives particularly Mrs. Greene—"in the mean time not forgetting the Dr".—

At last Mr. Bassett & I made a desperate plunge into another room, where we found Mama & various dignitaries. Talked to Mr Bassett, Mr. Tudor &c &c— The crowd meanwhile was immense & composed of every variety of the human species, from Mrs. Waterhouse in a cap, that I am firmly persuaded was a *bonnet de nuit*, up to Mrs Harry Otis, tossed off in a pink hat &c &c— You may imagine the sensation Mrs Otis created, in the assembly— I kept afar off— Talked to various personages—& viewed the motely group around us— Toward the end of the evening went into the other room—found various worthies I had never seen before—among them Edmund & Lucilla, & various people from town—Mrs. Gilman &c &c— Talked to Mr. Phillips, who really looked a little woke up and to Mr Johnson—

I then saw Mama departing—so I beckoned the arm of Mr Alvord to-wards me, & we glided out of the apartment. I ascended a staircase for the shawls of the rest of the party, & was lightly descending again, & spring-ing gracefully forward, when I heard a fearful rent, in my garments, & perceived that the fairy foot of Mr John Bethune had been planted upon my unhappy dress and nearly rent it in twain— His look of horror I shall not soon forget, & in spite of all I could say, persisted in declaring it to be irreparable— I however taking the arm of Mr Alvord passed onward leav-ing him to the stings of his own conscience.— We had certainly an amus-ing eveg—&, from Mama & Elisas description it seems to have been all very well managed. At home we found Cousin Nancy & Susan, who had had various people dotting in & out, & had had much amusement. We re-lated our experiences & then all sunk to our slumbers.—

Thursday 13th. Morning went to the Garden—looked delightfully. Walked about there some time—then left—Mrs Tracy & Elisa, at Mrs. Channings—& returned home. Sally Gardner came in, had *walked* from *Waltham*, asked her to dinner—accepted— Fixed flowers—& sent our usual bouquet to Frederic Hoffman—& then was so tired fell upon the bed, & went to sleep.— Was just dressed again when Mrs Hunt—Abby Phillips & Maria Hunt—Maria quite pretty & interesting—Mrs Tracy— Elisa & Miss Gardner returned to dinner— Had a very pleasant one.— Mr John Bromfield came in the aftrnoon, arousing as usual all the hapless sleepers. At 5 o'ck Susan & Mrs. Tracy—took Miss Gardner to Wal-tham.— Mr Snelling called. He happened to mention something about Massels exhibition,[13] & after he was gone Mama regretted very much that she had not thought of taking Cousin Nancy to see, it & we determined that if they returned time enough from their ride, she would take her in, that eveg— About half past six the carriage returned—the proposal was agreed to— The lame horse slipt out & papas slipt in— Tea hurried thro', & Mama, Papa, Mrs. Tracy & Elisa, whirled into town—being an appropriate finale to the varieties of this week.—

After their departure, we walked & talked till 8 o'ck—when we were joined by Henry Cleveland & Mr. Felton— Were conversing very pleasant-ly—when Mr Church made his entrée—introducing Mr Campbell—a gentleman from N. Carolina, who brought a letter from Mr Jones.— I had to entertain Mr Church—& a bad bargain I had of it—for never did I see him appear so boobyish, & disagreeable. We were very sorry they hap-pened in—as we should have had a much more agreeable eveg. with Henry, & Mr Felton— Mr Campbell is a lively, easy, Southerner, with a good deal of fluency—& ready conversation something à la Jones—only rather more *stable*, & not so handsome.— The gentlemen remained until ten—& soon after their excit, the Boston party returned. They had been entirely rewarded for their going in & appeared to have passed an amus-ing eveg.— We laughed & talked till a late hour.

Friday 14th. Immediately after breakfast Mama took Cousin Nancy & Elisa to Cambridgeport where they were to meet Mr Guild, who was to take Mrs Tracy to N.B Port. We bade her adieu with much regret—having enjoyed her visit exceedingly— Every thing has gone exactly right, & it has altogether been a very pleasant week.— Went to the [bath][14]— Messrs. Davis, Van Ranssellar & Chester—three Orthodox clergymen—rather pleasing—forget what we did the rest of the day.

Saturday 15— Morning drew &c believe no one came. Afternoon took a delightful drive.— Evening Mr. Sparks came was very agreeable—told us various anecdotes of John Randolph &c &c. Staid until nearly 12 o'ck.—

Sunday 16th Morning went to the Chapel— After church Sophia & I went to town to meet the returning travellers—paused in Chesnut St, & there remained until near the hour of three—listening to the distant wheels hoping that each would pause at the door— At lenght famishing friendship could no long wait but no sooner was dinner "set upon the table" than a loud ring at the door and—as you well remember—my dear Margy & Abby—your party arrived in safety—& were welcomed with sin-cere pleasure— Having brought my journal down to the hour of yr. ar-rival—I close my book—hoping that it may have afforded you some amusement.—

A. C. L. Q—

1833.[15]—

Sunday 16 June. Sophia & I went into town for Margy & Abby who arrived about 3 o'clk— After all the meetings were over & dinner discussed—& various little affairs arranged—we four ladies, departed at 5 o'clk for Cambridge— Had a pleasant drive, beguiling the way with various accounts— Greetings over with the travellers—we all talked & walked— Mr Hoffman (Uncle to Frederic) came— In the eveg. Mrss. Phipps & Thurston—& Mr Pierce.—

Monday 17th While we were at breakfast Lucilla came in, various exclamations— Margy & I decided to accompany her back to town— In a short time were on our way— Stopt at Chesnut St: where we passed the day in talking over all the various events of the last three months—& talk we did—& merrily did I laugh at Margys varied discriptions— In the evening Josiah, Tom Davis & Henry Cleveland came.—

Tuesday 18th Mama & Abby came in to town returned with them to Cambridge—wrote some notes for a small fête which we give tomorrow eveg. to Mrs Phillips.—

Wednesday 19th What we did in the morning past my feeble recollection— In the afternoon Mr. Robert Storer came, paid an agreeable visit, is certainly an excellent person. Margy & Mr Greene came out— After Mr Storers departure, dressed—for our evening fete— Mr & Mrs Quincy jr Mrs. Miller—Mrs Parker & Lucilla came from town—& a few Cambridge Ladies & agreeable gentlemen formed the circle— Talked to Mr Felton a long time—then to Rutledge, introduced him to Lucilla—then to Mr Campbell. Mary Jane sang—passed quite an agreeable evening all went off very well—wound up the eveg by a talk with Mr Church who was more absurd than ever.—

Thursday 20th Morning rained—afternoon went over to the Plains to see Louisa—found her quite sick—staid there some time—

Friday 21st Mama Susan & Sophia went into town to see the reception of Pres: Jackson. Abby & I walked & talked— On the return of the ladies had vivid sketches of the procession—all very elegant, appropriate & picturesque.

Saturday 22d Some idea that the President might visit Cambridge in the afternoon— Papa went in to ascertain—never sent out any word whether he was coming or not—left us in a happy state of uncertainty— Mama & Susan went in to town in the afternoon to see the Review— found that Papa had never thought of sending out any word— Abby & I talked & walked— Dr Follen dropt in— Evening: Ladies came home had—a most splendid time— Nothing ever seen like the beauty of the view, every thing as "fine as fivepence".—

Sunday 23d— fine day— Morning—did not go to church. Afternoon, all sunk to their slumbers—all the lower department went to Mr Newells—& all the higher department were profound, when I was aroused by a slight noise & on looking from my lattice discovered Mary Jane & Josiah scrambling out of a gig at the back door. I was so fast asleep that I could scarsely open the door— Met Mary Jane at the head of the stairs, who said she could only compare the house to a deserted castle: not a being to be seen, & dead silence reigning over it. Finding every one in this Castle of Indolence asleep[16]—she caught the spirit of the place & retired to sleep also—& Josiah followed her example. By church time however, all were awake, & all save Abby went to church, & heard a good sermon from Mr Henry Ware. Horace Cleveland came to tea—but soon after Mary Jane & J departed—

As it was expected that Pres: Jackson would visit Cambridge on Monday afternoon, various directions & arrangements were to be made— In a few moments however, Mrs Farrar enters, with an air of more than usual importance. "Where is Miss Susan," said she— "I know she is a sight seer, you young ladies are not I presume willing to go with me tomorrow at four o'clk to Charleston, to see the Constitution taken in to the Dock[17]—before the Pres: &c"— Abby arose to inform Susan—when Mrs. Farrar called after her that she must find her own conveyance as her carryall was full!— It appeared that Henry Davis had agreed to give her party a very good place, & that was the inducement— After much debate, of the how's & the when's, it was agreed that Susan & Abby should be at Mrs F's door at 4 o'clk—& then Mrs Farrar departed—

Just as this was arranged we discovered that Major Bacon was engaged to be at Charleston in his military capacity, which rather interfered with his civil duty of driving the carriage—here was a contre temps— The Major proposed that the *Sexton* Mr Lion, should take his place, but this idea was abandoned as the ladies had no wish to be driven by so ominous an attendant. So at last the Major gave up his own plans—as he was not obliged by *duty* to be there—& it was finally arranged. It then occurred to the ladies, that some attendant spirits might be necessary—& after various debates decided to ask Mr Beck & Mr Felton— A faculty meeting was in Papas library, & Mama made a bold attack upon the door & requested him to ask the two above named gentlemen to the parlour after the meeting— Accordingly they soon desended and are of course exceedingly happy to be included in the party, and so it was all arranged—

Just after the two attending Professors had bowed out, a note was brought in from Mrs Hill—desiring to know whether the ladies should come to our house the next day to be introduced to the President. This asking for invite, was deemed some what peculiar and a dire debate insued as we had just determined not to invite any ladies as he staid so short a time— However, as we must have the Hills we determined to ask the Valleys & their inhabitants also— Mama & I retired to indite a diplomatic note—to Mrs Hill—& heard various ringings at the bell—

After the note was despatched, desended & found Mr Alvord, Mr Wendell Phillips & Mr King in the parlour.— Mr Phillips was very agreeable, tho' it is a mystery how he came to favor us this evening as in general Man delights him not—nor woman either—but he was gentlemanly & agreeable that evening— Just as Mr Alvord & Mr Phillips departed, Mr Gardner & Mr May enter—

In the mean time various notes had been flying between Susan & Mrs Farrar, concerning the next morning—& now the sky was beginning to be over cast, & fears were entertained that the rain might drown all their plans— Notes were therefore despatched to Dr Beck & Mr Felton, to say that if it rained they must not trouble themselves to come— While all this was going on the two divines were quietly seated, conversing—Mr Gardner more singular than ever— During the evening Mr May begged him to sing some favorite air—not precisely suited to a Sunday evening—after closing the doors—& waiting some time he sings the two first lines—& then no power can persuade him to go on—acted very oddly—Mr May rather disconcerted—

Mama at this moment remembers that Papa was to speak to Mr Gardner & despatches a messenger for him— Gentlemen in the mean time know nothing of it—therefore take leave—are in the entry, when Papa rushes down— All return—discuss the music for the next day—in honor of President Jackson—at lenght arranged—gentlemen bow out for the last time— After their departure, laughed much at the absurdities of the day, & then after arranging the dresses & the *provisions* for the early flight the next day—retire to rest— Susan sleeps in nearly her whole toilette for fear of not being ready— About 12 ock all is silent.—

Monday 24th Awoke as I thought at midnight by Susan getting up—& Miranda, at the door. "Whats the matter" says I half asleep "Its half past

3," say Miranda—"but its raining as hard as it can." "We shan't go then certainly" says Susan, wandering to the window—exit Miranda. "Actually raining" says I— "glad its decided" says Susan (still at the window). "Theres a tall gentleman with an umbrella over his head going by. I dare say its Mr Felton"— A moment after—a loud & insulting barking is heard, from Driver & Leopard, assured us that they were saluting the Professors enterance into the grounds— Thought I should have died with laughter at the idea of poor Mr Felton arousing himself at ½ past 3 o'clk on a rainy morning to be received in this hospitable manner.— Horace's voice heard from his turret, first stilling the dogs, & then holding converse with the Professor— All parties at lenght satisfied & all return to forget their woes in oblivion.— At breakfast all laughed much over the events of the night or rather of the morning—

Then proceeded to arrange the rooms—& write notes to all the ladies asking them to come here in the afternoon— All just despatched, when a gig drives furiously to the door—letter to Papa brought in. Papas voice heard on the stairs exclaiming— Well—heres an end of it—heres an express to say that the President is too ill to leave his room—& cannot of course visit Cambridge to day!

Here was a "*catastroph*"! All up in the wind again— All preparations thrown away— All the invitations to be recalled— Began to write notes immediately— In the midst of it when the door opens, & in comes Gov Cass, (Secy of War) Mr Poinsett[18]— Mr Prentiss of the Army & Mr Wetmore.— Mama & I entered— Gentlemen expressed great reget that so many people were disappointed &c—paid a short visit & departed— Laughed much after they were gone at the Contretemps of the last two days—literally "full of sound and fury signifying nothing"— A beautiful basket of flowers entered from Mrs Webster— I seised upon some to wear to Mrs Goulds[19]—& we then rested from our labours—

In the afternoon Papa & I were just setting off for town— when Mr Hoffman & Ann—came in—talked some-time—asked Mr Hoffman to go to town with us, accepts— I go out to order the Carriage— Comes to the door— I give notice—behold to my surprise, Papa taking leave of Mr Hoffman—find that he has changed his mind—& is not going— Bows exchanged— Just exiting, when we fall over Mr John Pickering at the door— All return— Stay a few moments—ask Mr Pickering to ride in— he accepts—take leave again, & drive off— Mr Pickering & Papa very agreeable—had a very pleasant drive—

Left Mr P at his own house—then went to Chesnut St— Found Margy & Sophia in the parlour— Describe the varied absurdities of the last days— Sophia returns with Papa to Cambridge.— Mary Minot came in— looks very pretty had a long & agreeable visit from her— Then did up my hair—after tea dressed— at ½ past nine join Edmund & Lucilla, & drive to Mrs Goulds party for Mrs Wells—expected a dance— Lo! it is only a talking party—very agreeable however talked first to Mr Wolcott—Frank Shaw &—then to Frank Codman very agreeable—then a long time to Mr Robert Storer, in which we discussed various interesting topics— Mr. R.G. Shaw then came up—affectionate meeting—like him amasingly.— Mr Miers next very pleasant. Mrs Wells is a frenchified figure—very beautifully dressed—& rather pleasing— Took leave about 11 o'ck—passed a very agreeable eveg.—

Tuesday 25— Raining very hard. Staid in town— Margy quite sick— talked & read all day. Josiah came in the eveg.—

Wednesday 26— Aroused by Papas ring at the door—might have been heard in Greenland— Screamed upstairs that the President would be in Cambridge at 10 o'clk— Slam'd the door & drove off.— Dressed—& bd on their way to Charleston. The President is a very gentlemanly old man, but seems so feeble, that unless Mr Van Buren takes great care he may be King before next winter.— Some of the Company remained some time expressed much pleasure &c all went off exceedingly well—have not time to do justice to half the absurdities of the morning—a very pleasant one it was however.—

After all were departed, determined to go back to town with Edmund, as I was engaged to dine at Mrs Minots— Accordingly after a short disdegree of Dr of Laws was given &c &c all in the happiest manner.

At ½ past ten—the services were over— All the ladies came here—assembled in the dining room—save our own family. President soon entered with Papa—followed by his Suite—recieved by Mama, & seated by Mama on the Sopha— All the ladies then introduced, & then all the Collegians entered & passed before him—coming in at one door—& passing out at the other. Quite a scene—very well managed— Collection of people here beyond all enumeration— Asked Capt Morgan where Mr Van Buren was.[20] Points out a short man with red hair—flys off—& in a few moments returns with the aforesaid short man, & introduces him as "Mr Van Buren the *Vice* President" (in every sense of the word)

Mr Van Buren, just what I expected—very subdued in his manner—

hardly raised his eyes, talked in the most confidential tone of voice, all de-
votion to a lady— Asked me if I had been introduced to the President—
Said no, I had not—as there were so many demands on his attention—
Assured me that must not be—begged to be allowed to have the honor of
presenting him to me— Assented—but waited till the Collegians were
gone— Mr Van Buren assured me the only thing that had taken away
from the pleasure of this tour—was his *extreme* anxiety for the health of
the President! "Och the cratur!"

Just then crowd opened Mr Van Buren drew my arm into his & presented me to the President—shook hands with him & then gave way to the
others. Talked to a variety of people— Mr Van Buren insinuates himself
thro' the crowd—presses my hand & bids me farewell— President takes
leave of Mama— [Suite] of frights, ditto—& all bow out of the room—&
proceed on their way to Charleston. The President is a very gentlemanly
old man, but seems so feeble, that unless Mr Van Buren takes great care
he may be King before next winter.— Some of the Company remained
some time expressed much pleasure &c all went off exceedingly well—
have not time to do justice to half the absurdities of the morning—a very
pleasant one it was however.—

After all were departed, determined to go back to town with Edmund,
as I was engaged to dine at Mrs Minots— Accordingly after a short discussion of the morning—drove back to Boston— Went to Mr Parkers to
pass the time before dinner with Lucilla— All out however—& therefore
passed an hour & a half in solitary magnificence. Morning in Cambridge
seemed like a dream— Saw Lucilla for a few moments—& about three
o'clk when to Mrs Minots—Mary in the parlour— Soon joined by Henry
Davis—like him very much. Mrs Minot & Miss Freeman soon enter &
then Mr Walsh—a son of Mr W's of Phila. brother to the redoubtable
Robert.[21]— Very pleasing man—unaffected & easy—the most pleasing of
the family— Is in the Navy & has therefore acquired the openess of a
sailors manners— Went down to dinner with Henry Davis— Sat next Mr
Walsh—very pleasant— Mr Lee a Leut in the Army—came in while we
were at table—rather pleasing—

During dinner some thing is said about the Navy Yard— Mary & I say
we never saw it—are invited by Mr Davis to come at any time— Mrs Minot
thinks no time so good as the present, & proposes to ajourn to Charleston
after dinner— all agree—to so agreeable a plan— Messenger dispatched
for the largest carriage to be procured. (Mentally said with Tom Davis/

"hope its) a stout one"— At 5 o'clk a carriage of portentous sise comes to the door—borrowed a bonnet of Mary—& all desend.— Mrs Minot, Miss Freeman—Mary—myself, Mr Davis & Mr Walsh all get in —& off we go.—

Afternoon delightful. Had a very pleasant drive—went first to Bunker Hill—all dressed for the Presidents visit—triumphal arches, flags—evergreens &c & the monument covered with people, & the flags flying from every corner. All got out, stiff breese blowing—ascend to the top of the monument— Wind blew my dress directly over my head— Henry Davis held it down with his walking stick—beautiful view—I mean *from* the monument. Admired & sentimentalised for some time. Made some apt quotation about the "banner not yet torn",[22] which was waving over us— Looked up and saw a great rent in it—no matter— Walked to the other side—laughed at various oddities, & then desended— Got in to the carriage, drove to the gate of the Navy Yard— All got out, fight between two horses— Carriage & gig locked together every body dreadfully frightened—flew into the Navy Yard, never saw the end of it.— Walked on with Henry Davis, who had Mrs Minot on his other arm.

Went first to the Dock. The old ship Constitution now lying in it being repaired— Scrambled on board of her—fine vessel— Sailors clearing out the hold—looked, & sounded like so many demons— Walked about the ship some time— then went over the dock—down into it—was very much struck by the beauty contrivance & magnitude of the work— It is really sublime—that little insignificant Man, could plan & execute such works, seemed almost incredible.

Leaving the Dock, walked to the Columbus—which is the ship Mr Davis is stationed at—Immense—74— Clambered up the side—pulled in to the side of the vessel by a youth in uniform— Mr Davis introduced as Leut. Hasard. All promenaded the deck, [went] above about, & underneath fine display of ankles— Ship far exceeded my expectations for sise & convenience. Heard Mr Davis, despatch "Constantine the Steward" to see if the ladies could go into his state room. Went into the room where the gentlemen dine—very nice—all the ship looked as neat as possible— Constantine seen coming out of the state room, where I presume he had cleared the decks a little— Mr Davis vanishes into it also—& in a few moments returns—invites us to enter— All ajourn—

State room quite large—much better place than I had supposed— All sat down, while Mr Davis sat on the side of his cot, & played on the guitar— Odd enough to be sure it seemed— Mr Hasard quite gentlemanly— as all sailors are— Remained there some time—then bade Mr Hasard good eveg—as he being on duty, could not leave the ship.—

Scrambled down to the wharf—& then walked to the great Ship of War, which is built under the house—never yet launched— Went all over it— What a monster it is—beautifully built—quite delighted with it— Walked up & down the deck with Mr Walsh—explained various parts of it— Naval fever quite warm this afternoon— left the great ship, & then went to the storehouses— Went to the sail loft—saw some beautiful models of different ships— Messrs. Walsh & Davis explained the different parts—told me the names of the ropes—went over my lesson to Mr Walsh—called "the fore swifter" "the *back shifter*"²³—took all his sailor gallantry to keep from a shout of laughter— Came down from my high ropes—& followed the rest of the party down stairs— Went into the Magasine—saw the arms &c—a cutlass boarding pikes &c &c. Went also to the rooms where the sailors clothes were being packed—nice as wax— Left the Store house & after a few more turns, returned to the Carriage. Had a very pleasant visit to the Navy Yard. Do not know when I have passed a pleasanter afternoon—had a pleasant drive home—

During something said about the Concert that eveg—Mr Walsh & Mr Davis going—wanted Mary & me to go with them— Should like to very much but believed Mama would send in for me at six—was told it was then near 7 o'clk— Stopt at Mrs Minots—all got out. Sat at window with Mr Walsh— Our carriage drove up— Nobody in it—went down— Horace said Abby was at Chesnut St. got in—was screamed to by Henry Davis & Mr Walsh from the balcony to come back again— Drove to Chesnut St. found Abby & Edmund there— Asked Abby to stay—go with us to the Concert— Nothing she would like better, but Mr Gardner had come in the morning to say that if we were disengaged he would come to sing in the eveg— So she had flown in, to ask Mary Jane to come out & to bring me out also.

Here was a dilemma. Scotch music & Mr Gardner—Italian music & the Concert—dire was the debate— Abby got in to the carriage & back we went to Mrs Minots—got out loud talking—at last decided for the Concert— Abby departed solus—& I ascended to Marys apartment to fix my hair— Arranged in a few moments—hurried tea over—& Mr Davis & Mary Mr Walsh & myself—sat off—

Had a very pleasant walk to the Masonic Hall— thought the Concert was to begin at 8 o'clk—& therefore went as fast as possible— Reach'd the Hall flew upstairs—threw open the door—& lo! not more than ten people there— Found that we were half an hour too early— Took our seats however, talked & laughed with Mr Walsh & Frank Codman, who sat behind me. Concert began— Signora sang delightfully— All very fine voices—"first rate"—but as I am not sufficiently skilled in the science of music to appreciate it properly cannot therefore be a judge— Had much pleasure in hearing it however, & the skill with which they sang was astonishing— One bass voice was really *stunning* as Frank Codman says[24]—

Had a pleasant evening— Walked home by moonlight— The Common & mall, with the moon shining in the pond & on the distant country was exquiste.— Mr Walsh walked home with me— All went in to Mrs Minots—sat round the table laughing & talking until nearly twelve— Gentlemen then took leave—and Mary & I retired to our apartment and laughed over the various thing I had done & seen that day—but we were so fatigued that we were soon asleep—

Thursday 27th Came down to breakfast in my light silk—quite à la heroine—Mary half asleep— All at breakfast—had a pleasant one— It being a rainy morning—Mary Miss Freeman & I sat in the parlour & worked & talked— Mrs Minot came in with a note from Henry Davis— which she said was directed to her, but presumed it was intended for the young ladies— Dated from his State room on board the Columbus very pretty note indeed— Truly Mrs Minot did not do it justice— Some morning visitors came in—& about 1 o'ck the carriage came— Bade Mrs Minot & Mary adieu— Thanked them for the agreeable time I had passed with them—& drove away having had a very pleasant visit.—

Found Abby, Margy, & Sophia in the Carriage. The Concert at our house the preceeding eveg appeared to have been amusing & pleasing Mr Gardner, Mr Phipps—Mr Dwight & Mr Pattison & Miss Quincy, the performers—Mr and Mrs Phillips Mr Harrington & the family audience— Songs without number sung— Much amusement from the Lady Margys accounts.— Afternoon read loud in the journals— In the eveg—Papa brought out the sad intelligence George Davis' death—news of which has just been received[25]— It is indeed a stroke little expected and to his poor Mother irreparable.—

Friday 28th Morning—Mama Abby & Margy were going to Dedham— thought I would go over & pass the day with Louisa— Went accordingly— Stopt at the Plains, found Louisa gone to pass the day in town— So went on to Dedham— Found Aunt better. Place looked most lovely. Walked about—eat & slept & played with the baby— Left Abby to spend a few days there— Had a very pleasant drive into town— Went to Cousin Susans— Mrs Bliss came down—said that Mrs Davis was rather more composed—but the blow had been almost more than she could support— Mama went up to see her, & passed some time with her— Mr Davis seems almost as much overwhelmed—but there is no grief like the grief of a Mother.—

After staying there a long time, came out of town—found various people had been here—& Sophia related various of her adventures— A small party at Mrs Ed Channings was to be attended— Felt but small inclination to attend—but went at 9 o'ck with Papa & Susan— Small party—& dreadful derth of beaux—not a young gentleman there except Wm. Channing! Talked to him a long time & then to Mr Johnson— Edward Channing very amusing— Mr Farrar very agreeable.— Passed quite a pleasant eveg.—

Saturday 29th Morning all went to town save Sophia & I— drew &c walked up to Mrs Cragies to call on Mrs Sparks & Miss Johnson a lady who is staying there— Mrs Sparks is indeed a lovely creature, & is almost the only lady to whom that hacknied term can be applied with truth. Miss J. rather pleasing— After our return—Mrs Guild & Mr and Mrs Channing came.— All returned to dinner—various adventures— brought Lucilla out to pass Sunday here.

Afternoon—Mr Robert Storer came—very agreeable— Soon after Mr Jona Phillips & Wm enter—a take leave—before going to Europe— All sink down by respective talkers— Something very *real* about Mr Storer— like him very much— Mr Phillips seemed really animated with the idea of going—& took leave with many affectionate messages.— Mr Storer remained a short time after Mr Phillips departure, & then bowed out. Towards evening Sophia & Lucilla—Margy & I walked to the Botanic Garden— met with various adventures. Garden looked delightfully—had a pleasant walk— Eveg. Edmund came out.—

Sunday June 30th— fine day— Mr Wells dined here— wrote all day.— Horace Cleveland drank tea here. Henry Cleveland, Mr & Mrs Phillips Mr Beck, Mr Campbell, Mr Church, Mr Felton, & Mr Newell the eveg visitors— Talked to Mr Campbell,—quite gentlemanly & knows a thing or two— Staid till we nearly fell from our chairs.— Mr Church *conversed* most of the eveg with *Papa*, would have given *fourpence* to know what he was saying— Papa thinks him a *sensible* young man!!!!—

CHAPTER 5

The Places in Anna Quincy's Life

July & August 1833

In July and August Anna frequently strolled around the Harvard campus, made excursions to Mt. Auburn and the Botanical Garden, and visited friends in Cambridge. She traveled by carriage to Boston twelve times, walking to various sites in the city, and went to Quincy for six days in July. Rare was the day when Anna wrote, "Staid home all day." In a journal with almost continuous movement, these three places—Cambridge, Boston, and Quincy—dominate. Because her family's wealth provided ownership of a carriage, Anna could suddenly decide that she wished to be in Boston; less affluent Cambridge residents, however, had to take a one-hour bus (stagecoach) trip, and Harvard undergraduates frequently made the trip on foot. The home on Boston's prestigious Chesnut Street, where Anna's sister Margaret and her husband, Benjamin Greene, lived, served as the convenient city residence for the family. Thus Anna thought nothing of crossing the Charles River in the family's carriage to visit a friend in Boston, attend a party, or, having stayed in Boston, return to Cambridge for an evening with the family. She might also accompany a member of the family to tend an ailing relative in Quincy.

Although only a few miles apart, Boston and Cambridge represented different social environments. In Boston, then a city of 61,400 residents, Anna shopped and attended plays, concerts, art exhibits, and charity fairs. In Cambridge, a village of about 6,000, she enjoyed the rural delights of the Botanical Garden—including an encounter with several cows on 7 August. Cambridge life for Anna was naturally dominated by the family's duties to receive faculty and students. Boston meant cotillions and elegant dinners in Beacon Hill mansions; but Cambridge meant only "talking parties" and sometimes a "great dearth of grown up gentlemen."

The small village of Quincy, named for Anna's ancestors when it had separated from the town of Braintree in 1792, provided still another contrast. Anna cherished this summertime retreat at the 1770 Quincy mansion, remembering "the joy of going to Quincy," a focus of the extended family activity and, in 1886, "now a life quite passed away."[1] Her July stay there produced only brief diary entries; this quietly satisfying country visit lacked both the stimulus of Boston and the sociability of Cambridge.

Thus the world of the 1833 diary is a circumscribed, if lively, one. Anna views the intrusion of events beyond her circle as noteworthy, for example, the Niagara Falls trip on 24 July, when, quoting Psalms, she writes that others in the family "take the wings of the morning." Even farther removed is New Orleans, where, the former Harvard law student Jesse Harrison tells her, duels are fought and "Death is so common . . . that life is scarsely regarded" (19 August). Anna expresses surprise that this young man "intended taking up his abode for a month or two in *Cambridge*," after savoring excitements elsewhere (6 August).

Life outside the United States manifests itself to Anna primarily through British literature, as her references to the works of Shakespeare, Byron, and Scott, besides of course Austen, indicate. The long tale by a Mr. Campbell of North Carolina about the exploits of the British adventurer Edward Trelawny leaves her impressed but skeptical. Although intrigued with this report of Trelawny's friendship with Byron, she writes, "The *marriage* & the *Shark*, are two points in the story that some what shake my credulity" (18 August). In contrast with her attraction to British literature, Anna rarely refers here either to American literature or to continental works in translation. In this vein, she notes with fascination and at times some intimidation those visitors from foreign countries outside the British Isles, as we saw in her entry of 25 May regarding the "little oddity," a child of the German scholar Therese Robinson, who speaks "this unknown tongue." The sudden appearance of a Chinese servant at the Forbeses' residence is "really electric" (19 July). She wants others to know that the Italian Marquis Charles Torrigiani has entered the narrow realm of Cambridge, writing when she finds his calling card, "We laid them on the table however to have it known that we knew a Marquis" (12 August).

Recording the "take leaves" of many visitors departing on European tours, Anna worries at times that travel abroad might taint young men such as Dutton Russell, who had called on 6 May: "On parting I begged Mr Russell not to be too overpowering on his return, & told him that an unaffected travelled gentleman would be a delightful novelty." On 20 May she described Henry Cleveland, upon his return from Europe, as "'quite a dandy'— Hat in hand, frockcoat on back, and whiskered cheek—quite a foreign tournure, & vastly improved." A summertime conversation with

Jesse Harrison persuades her that Europe could cause ruin as much as "improvement": "he thought a tour to Europe was a very doubtful good for a young man. . . . 'a visit to Europe, Miss Quincy changes the views, opinions & feelings of a young man so entirely—that on his return he can hardly be considered as the same person'"(9 August). Thus, for Anna Europe's impact on character can be both beguiling and threatening.

Nor are her reservations about life beyond the Boston area confined to young men. On 11 June, after reading her sister Margaret's letter from a steamboat somewhere in the southern United States, Anna wrote, "You really seem determined to get your *joltings* worth." She anticipated then her sister's travel through Europe and the Middle East until Margaret would ultimately "'penetrate into the central regions of Africa, & thence, right onward, till you are unexpectedly bounded by the sea at the Cape of Good Hope,' & I hope at last the mysterious 'nods of a manderin of the Court of China,' will give you a faint glimmering of the propriety of spending the rest of your days in New England.—" The young Anna Quincy remained content to voyage only vicariously, via literature and travelers' observations. Cambridge, Boston, and Quincy provided a universe wide enough for her.

Sketch of a pond at Mt. Auburn, 1837. "Walked all over Mt Auburn. Truly romantic & mysterious—the dark woods, the white monuments dimly seen thro' the uncertainly light among the trees—half eclipsed moon, sheding a disastrous twilight over the scene on one side, & a distant pile of dark clouds on the other, from which bright flashes of lightening were seen to play.— Altogether a most beautiful & striking scene, one not easily forgotten" (1 July 1833). Quincy Papers, Massachusetts Historical Society.

July & August 1833

Monday 1st of July— Lucilla went to town immediately after breakfast— Mama & Sophia also
went in— We read, talked &c Miss Randall was
the only visitor— Weather very warm—almost
melted.— Afternoon—Mr & Mrs Cranch Mrs
Blind Greenleaf came— Mama took them up to
Mt Auburn, almost died in the effort the heat so
intense— Mr Swaith joined them at tea—also
Henry Parker, & Horace Cleveland. about 8 o'ck—
Sophia, Margy, Horace C. & myself went up to see
Mt Auburn by moonlight— Lo & behold—moon
almost totally eclipsed! had a delightful drive—
Walked all over Mt Auburn. Truly romantic & mysterious—the dark woods, the white monuments
dimly seen thro' the uncertainly light among the
trees—half eclipsed moon, sheding a disastrous
twilight over the scene on one side, & a distant
pile of dark clouds on the other, from which
bright flashes of lightening were seen to play.—
Altogether a most beautiful & striking scene, one

not easily forgotten— Wandered over the whole ground very delightfully— Passed a *refreshing* eveg.—

Tuesday 2d Wrote to Miss Pomeroy— Mr Hoffman & Ann, dined
here— It is decided that they leave Cambridge on Thursday—take Frederic to Baltimore, & probably send them both to Europe as soon as he is
well enough, to meet their parents— Of all the short histories on the
records of the changing scene of Cambridge the Hoffmans seem to be the
most fleeting. They seem to have just come to interest all our feelings &
then we lose sight of them forever— If Frederic only recovers—we should
be entirely selfish to regret his leaving us so soon— But to a being like
him, "it will be well—whether life or death is his portion"[2]— Ann
seemed to feel a good deal at the idea of leaving Cambridge—as much as
could be expected from one so young.— Mr Hoffman is a complete man
of the world & very gentlemanly— Has been devoted to Frederic, & seems
to be very much attached to them both.—

Afternoon—Mr McLellan called, a youth of the class of 1829, (one recommendation at least) who has just returned from the tour of Europe—
tho' I had presumed he was safely deposited in Boston all the time. Paid a
long visit—described various wonders of nature & art—& departed—
After tea Mrs Keating & Augustus came.—

Wednesday 3d Rained very hard—intended to have gone to town to
bring out Lucilla, but the weather prevented— Judge Pierce of Gloucester,
& a Mr Page came, & soon after in a pouring rain, up drives a carriage & 3
ladies & a gentleman alight— Prove to be Mrs Boyleston—Mr & Mrs Curtis, & young Mrs Curtis. I did not know them from *Adam*—& coming
down after their arrival, & nobody introducing me, we smiled, & smiled,
& were none the wiser.— Did not remain long. Rain poured down all day
which we regretted on Mrs Cragie's account, who was to have a party that
eveg. & the moon considered a most important attendant— However, the
rain came down—as if it had never rained before & never intended to rain
again—

At ½ past 7 Mama, Papa, Sophia, I drove to Mrs Cragies—thro' midnight dark— After various twistings & turnings, & openings & shutings
of the door, drove to the side of the Piassa, & thereby escaped being
drowned. House all lighted up—looking very finely— Went upstairs to
take off our cloaks. Were received in Mrs. Cragies parlour— Took a tour
of the rooms with Richard Fay, who looked extremely handsome—concluded by going in to the dancing room, & dancing. Not very pleasant—

Great dearth of grown up gentlemen— When dance concluded Mr Robert Storer, came up—took his arm & wandered over the house for the next hour. Very gentlemanly—continue to like him— Talked a little while to Mr Sparks—then danced with Mr Storer—not a Vestris it must be confessed. 3 Went in to Supper with him— Almost crushed— Returned to the dancing room—was going to dance with Mr Alvord—but departed before the dance commenced. Passed quite a pleasant eveg.—

Thursday 4th Morning, Mama Sophia & Margy went to Quincy— I walked up to see Mrs Sparks, & took Copley Greene's miniature with me much admired.— Mrs Sparks very pleasing.— After my return the Miss Park's called.— Quincy party did not return until late.—

Friday 5th Fine day— Ann Hoffman called early to bid us adieu—they were to leave Cambridge at 10 o'clk, & take an easy journey to Providence. Ann looked very pretty & seemed to feel a good deal at leaving us. It was thought best that no one should see Frederic, before he went, as any excitement was injurious to him. Ann bade us adieu, carrying with her many good wishes, & we indeed feel grieved & disappointed that thus ends all the plans that had been formed for our two interesting young friends but it is vain to regret what we cannot controul.—

Mama & I soon after went to town, as we left our door, the stage was before Mrs Curtis', & Ann & Frederic, just getting in— it drove off—and with it all the bright promises, all the hopes, the interests & the affection, which Frederic Hoffman had excited— their recollection remained however, and will long be cherished—and with tearful eyes, we caught the last glimpse of those who had interested us so deeply— It seems now like a dream that we have known them,—and this is a sad waking—but so it must be, and in Cambridge of all places, we should become accustomed to these changes, but this is a peculiar case which brings with it feelings which are rarely excited, & cannot be surpressed.—

Mama & I proceeded to town went first to Cousin Susans— Passed some time with her— She appears extremely well—& makes the greatest efforts to command herself—though it is plain how deep her grief is. After leaving her went up to Mrs Salisburys— Change of scene & feeling—only saw Mrs S—talked on various subjects— Mama called for me & we went home, taking Lucilla with us to pass a few days.— In the afternoon Mrs Johnson, Cousin Nancy Storer & Mr Templeton Johnson came.—

Saturday 6th delightful day— Lucilla & I took a walk after breakfast then talked & worked, until 12, when Margy & I went to call on Mrs Beck— Saw her & Abby.— On our return found Mrs Sparkes & Miss Johnson—Mrs Gorham Brooks & Mrs Charles Adams in the parlour— Ladies very pretty & agreeable.— Afternoon Miss Willard came. Soon after Mr Walsh & Wm Swett came in— Having rode out on horseback—they seemed absolutely melted, & Mr Walsh scarsely recovered his equilibrium while here—however appeared very well & is pleasing. Wm Swett as distracted as ever.— After their departure Mr. J Pickering & Mr Folsom came.— Eveg. Mama returned from Dedham bringing Abby home.—

Sunday 7th Felt like every thing, did not go to church. Lost a most admirable Sermon from Mr H. Ware— Horace Cleveland drank tea here. Mrs Crafts, the amiable George Mr Felton & Mr Swett came.—

Monday 8th Very warm—all went to town in the morng—save Lucilla Mama & myself— Afternoon—forget what we did

Tuesday. 9— Papa went to Dedham, brought word that Aunt Dowse was ill— Mama & Susan went over there in the afternoon. Mrs Higginson came—eveng—talked &c—

Wednesday 10th Morning, Lucilla & I walked went to the bath &c— Mrs & Mrs. Coit came— Afternoon, Mrs Parker, Mr & Mrs & Miss Francis—came— Mrs Peck also dropt in— In the eveg—Messrs Whitney & Lovering.—

Thursday 11th Morning walked. Mrs Fay & Mrs R. Fay came.— Afternoon—forget what we did.

Friday 12— All went to town except Margy & me— We walked & paid various visits—almost blown away— In the eveg—Margy & I went to Mrs Dr Higginsons— Arrived early, & paid a visit to them before any other company arrived. House very pretty & every thing in very pretty taste. About 20 people there—mostly their own family— Talked to young Nichols a long time— Miss Davis sang, & to my amusement struck up Pinkney's serande—found that it had been printed— Mr Gardner then arrived—& we had various duo's—&—very fine. Mr Gardner, one of the greatest oddities, we have yet seen in Cambridge. Passed a very pleasant evening.—

Saturday 13th Morning walked with Lucilla— About 11 o'ck Abby Lucilla & I, drove to Medford to call on Mrs G. Brooks—had a pleasant drive—found Mrs B at home— Very pleasing indeed— Took us all over the place, which was in fine order & looked delightfully— Paid a very agreeable visit. Then drove across the country to Mr Cushing's— Gates closed, & neither Mr nor Mrs Cushing visible to view—left cards & sped homewards. Passed a very pleasant morng.

Afternoon—Mrs Newell called, to invite to a fête there, on Monday eveg— Politely declined— Mr Robert Storer our next visitor—agreeable & gentlemanly as usual— Mr & Mrs A Everett & Mrs Hale came. Mrs Crafts drank tea here— Mr Gardner, Mr Phipps & Mr Dwight in the eveg— Some delightful music. Mr Gardner sang some Scotch song, really exquistely— He sings in so finished a style with so much taste, & execution, that it is indeed a great pleasure to hear him— Several of the trios were very fine—particularly "To Greece we give our shining blades" which did indeed recall the first summer we passed here. 4 Heard of the Hoffmans safe arrival.

Sunday 14th Went to Mr Newells in the morng—dreadfully warm day—rained in the eveg— No one came.

Monday 15th Sick all day— Lucilla went home. Mr & Mrs Cranch, Mr Elliot & young Cranch dined here— Mr Campbell came in the evg— No one attended the Exhibition—

Tuesday 16th felt better— None of the ladies went to the Class oration, having no particular wish to hear Mr D. Webster[5]— None there fore appeared in the parlour—

Wednesday 17th Mama & I went over to Quincy—found Sophia & Mrs Miller at home— Mama remained there the rest of the day & night— Place looked delightful.—

Thursday 18th Mama & Sophia left us soon after breakfast remained with Mrs M.— read &c &c all day—towards evening Mrs C Adams came—

Friday 19th Mrs Thayer—a friend of Mrs Millers dined with us—very pleasing & interesting something like Aunt Jackson.— Mr Revere came. Took her home in the evening—had a pleasant drive— Went to Milton hill to call at Mrs Forbes's— Green blind door closed. Howe made an attack upon it—in a few moments it flew open with a violent jerk, & out came, a Chinese, in full costume white short *gown*, bare arms—long hair &c. The effect was really electric, & even Howe gave something like a start— The apparition not being able to speak English vanished again, & sent a woman to bear our names, as Mrs F was not at home— Presume it was an attendant of Mr. Bennets— Saw Mr B's fine new house—quite a sublime affair.[6] Had a pleasant drive home.—

Saturday 20. Mrs Miller went to town & I endeavour'd to entertain Josy during her absence. Got thro' the day with only two fits of roaring— But remembering how often the house had resounded to my own screams, I had more patience with my nephew.— Mrs M. returned about six — Soon after her return, a carriage drove up—& Mrs Forbes & Emma alighted— Various absurdities occurred during their visit.—

Sunday 21st Mama & Papa came over to Quincy before church. Mama told me the new plan of Susan & Sophia accompanying Papa to Niagara this week— All went to church— Mr Brooks preached— After church exchanged greetings with the Quincy world— The Peturbed rushed forward & armed me to the carriage.[7] In the afternoon—all went save Mrs Miller.— Mr Brooks as uninteresting as well could be— Attention some what distracted by a form in Mr Whitneys pew, which I at first thought was Mr Hill, Miss Carolines attendant, but who bore a strong likeness to Luther Angier— After church, we encountered in the porch, & I found it was he—'twas himself—but just as we were exchanging a few words— The Peturbed again rushed forth seised my hand & bore me away— Brought Mr & Mrs Cranch down to the place— Had a very pleasant visit from them.— Mama returned after tea.—

Monday 22d Excessively warm— Did nothing remarkable.—

Tuesday 23d Cooler— Mrs Miller, Josy & I paid some Quincy visits— On our return found notes from Cambridge— The party to Niagara joined by Lucilla & Mr Greene— All going off on Thursday— Mrs Miller kindly offered to bring me in to town that afternoon which I accepted— Had a very pleasant drive. Was set down in Chesnut St. Went up to Lucilla's—found her in the bustle of preparation—talked some time— Then went down in town for some things for her. Wanted to go to Edmunds office to ask him to drive me out to Cambridge. Men longing about in State St—did not like to go down without a gentleman— Met Mr Bassett asked him to go with me—of course flattered & happy—trotted down State St. & up to E's office, who was all amasement at the sight of me & Mr B— Decided to go out with me—

Walked back to Beacon St, & then came out of town— Horse the most wretched animal, seemed hardly able to put one foot before the other, & tumbled down several times— Sun shining directly in our faces—laughed much at the absurdity thereof however.— Edmund left me at the door & drove back again— Walked upstairs— All amased at the sight of me— where I had come from, & how I had got here. All engaged in packing & preparing— Laughed & talked—

Eveg— Mr. Felton came— Soon after Mr Campbell— Mr C quite a gentlemanly young man. Nothing very deeply interesting however. Staid till we nearly fell from our chairs.—

Wednesday 24th— Tremendously warm—packing & preparing all day—refreshing thunder shower in the afternoon. In the eveg—Papa Susan & Sophia bade us adieu, & were wafted into town, where they take the wings of the morning,[8] & flee away for Niagara.—

Thursday 25th Cool delightful day.— Mama & I went to town. Drove first to Chesnut St—Margy there— Travellers went off in fine Spirits— Went up to Marthas— Paid a long visit to Mrs Salisbury, Martha gone out— Then paid various visits—a long one to Elisabeth Grant— Sentimental as usual.— Then went back to Marthas— Still out— Staid till one o'clk, & then went to Chesnut St. & all came out of town. Afternoon Dr Flint came, & in his train two ladies & a gentleman who proved to be a Mr and Mrs Chartrain from Cuba—& a Miss Cook of Boston—the latter lady very handsome— Mrs C. very plain & very dark but quite pleasing— Abby went with them to the Library—. After tea Mrs Salisbury, Martha & Edward came—paid a flying visit— Eveg. Edmund came out.—

Friday 26— Mama went to Dedham—Margy & I to the bath.— Met Mrs Pierce, Miss Mills that was there— Mr Appleton & Mrs Appleton called. Afternoon Mr and Mrs Dunn, & Mrs Tom Phillips called. After tea Abby & I were tempted by the fineness of the evening to take the dust on the evening breese.— As we went round the corner, saw Judge & Mrs Story going in to the Law building—joined them & went in also[9]— Went all over the building— Such associations! After we left it—walked a short distance but the dust was really intolerable.— Mama & Edmund returned about 8 o'ck—left Aunt much the same.—

Saturday 27th Morning paid visits—went to Mrs Fay—saw Mrs F— Mrs R. F, & the baby[10] the latter is neither a fay or a fairy—but a fine little animal— The ladies quite agreeable. Afternoon Mr Felton— Eveg Edmund came out— Heard that Mr Alvord was ill— E. went in to see him— found him rather better—

Sunday 28th— Mr Lowell preached all day—very interesting indeed.— Mr & Miss Wells dined here—very pleasant & agreeable people.— Abby & Edmund went over to Quincy to pass the day— Edmund returned in the eveg—leaving Abby there.—

Monday 29th Heard sad news of Mr Alvord, who is very ill— Sent to Mrs Newells—found he was rather better. Then sent Horace to learn when the Steeple of the New Church was to be raised, & to ask Mr Sumner, the Law Student, to let us come over to the Law school to see it[11]— In a few moments Mama Margy & I, ajourned through the college grounds to the Law school, where Mr Sumner joined us— This youth, tho' altogether one of the least handsome personages I ever saw is such a good hearted, off hand, clever creature that it is impossible not to like him.[12] He took us all over the building, even into his own apartment, (*as he abides there all the time, being librarian*)—

We then took seats in Judge Storys room, to await the going up of the Steeple, which truly seemed in no hurry to arise. Presently *voices* are heard, & Mrs Story & two Miss Hills enter. They however decide to go below, & take seats on the portico— Mama joins them, while Margy & I remained at the window above, & amused ourselves with listening to the conversation below which the talkers had not "the remotest idea" we could hear. At lenght we are summoned to desend, as the ladies are going over to the church to see the machinery— Over we accordingly plunge—picking up the Divinity Student Mr Osgood, on the way. Before we reach the other side however—Mrs Story tells me that Judge Story charged her not to go near the church, for fear of some accident, & she thinks she is very wrong to go on— Pray turn back then, said I, I will return with you— While we hesitated, who should we see but the Judge himself, hurrying across— back we scampered, & met him on the way—

After telling us we were very wrong—he sends us back to the Law School, while he goes in search of Mama. They quickly returned, & we all seated ourselves on the Portico of the Law School. And truly we must have presented a singular spectacle to the passersby—whose astonishment at the apparition of this row of female forms, seated out on this public building without any obvious meaning, except the pleasure of taking the dust, & being seen by the passing travellers was not attempted to be concealed—

Two men I shall not soon forget, who passed in a gig— Their eyes I really fear suffered from the straining gase they directed towards us & as far as we could see them both heads were stretched out of the back of the gig to survey our picturesque group— And I suppose any passing Mrs Royal will set it down in black & white that it is the custom, for the Ladies in Camb. to pass the morning in the Porticoes of the public buildings!— The steeple meanwhile did *not* "grow a head" a minute but was such an everlasting time going up—that at last Mama & Margy who were going to

Harvard University, Cambridge, Mass. "Afternoon talked & worked—until 6—& then went forth to walk in the college grounds—proceeded onwards, & went down 'the sainted sod' of divinity Hall—" (31 July 1833). This 1830 drawing features University Hall at right center, where Anna Quincy frequently attended chapel services and where President Andrew Jackson received his honorary degree. Dane Law School, from which Anna and others watched the raising of the church steeple on 29 July, was located to the right of University Hall (not visible in this drawing). Engraving by Fenner, Sears and Co., courtesy of the Massachusetts Historical Society.

Dedham, departed— I staid with Mrs Story until it was finally fixed, & a beautiful Steeple it is— Had much amusement at various oddities.— Mr Sumner walked home with me arm in arm! Afternoon passed alone—save a short visit from Mr Sumner, to bring intelligence of Mr Alvord, which was less favorable.— Mama & Margy returned after tea. Edmund came out in the eveg—received Susans letter from on board the Steamboat.

Tuesday 30th rained all day—worked—drew—& read loud in Margys journal— Afternoon cleared off and Mama & I in the carriage & Margy on horseback took a pleasant ride.— Evening Mr Felton called—"quite pleasant" Edmund also comes out.

Wednesday 31st Fine day— Morning Mama went to Quincy, & from thence to Dedham to stay all night.— Margy & I were tête à tête all day— About 12, I sallied forth, to pay visits—went first to Dr Becks—front door open—saw various packages in the entry—& heard an odd knocking noise in the parlour— Asked whether Miss Phillips was at home— Woman hesitated—but asked me to walk in, entered & found Dr & Mrs B. engaged—in playing *backgammon*! Odd occupation for the lady & gentleman of the house at 11 o'ck in the morning— Thought it would have made a good story for the scandalous— Lady appeared embarrassed— Gentleman, seemed excessively amused. Board pushed aside, & visitor carefully avoided looking that way—at the same time saw every thing— Abby soon desended, & I paid a short visit & departed.—

Then proceeded accross the street to Dr Plymptons to call on Mrs Pierce. Made desperate attacks upon three different enterances before I found the right one, certainly it cannot be said of the Plymton mansion that there "is *no back door, to creep out of*".— Was at last ushered upstairs to a very pretty parlour—where I found Mr & Mrs Pierce—she reading the other writing—both appeared very well—but do not think Mrs P. any thing remarkable. After leaving them returned home, & joined Margy, & we departed to call upon an old Mrs. Robbins (mother of Dr R, who we heard was in Camb. & been told that it would be charity to go & see). On the way met Mr Sumner, who walked with us—told us Mr Alvord was better & that his father mother & sister had arrived.— Made various searches for Mrs Robbins' abode—but in vain & was obliged at last to give it up.—

Afternoon talked & worked—until 6—& then went forth to walk in the college grounds—proceeded onwards, & went down "the sainted sod" of divinity Hall— Caught some of the [divines] in a carryall, going like mischief—& Mr Gardner, running in the most unclerical manner— Eveg.

beautiful—delightful walk. Just as we were desending to tea, Horace Cleveland walked in—and we knew that he had come out to take a moonlight walk with us— Said nothing therefore about our previous rambles—but with the fortitude of martyrs gave our smiling congratulations on the fineness of the eveg.

After tea sat in the parlour till the moon rose— Horace said that Henry was also in Cambridge & was going to take a moonlight flitting to Mt Auburn with Miss Coffin—Ruinous name certainly. We three at last sallied forth, & again bent our steps towards the College grounds. Moonlight "absolutely splendid." As we were dodging down Prof: row, a tall figure is seen advancing— as he meets us, the moonlight fell upon his fine features, & Horace exclaimed in the most theatrical tone "Henry!" This was truly fine—but "Henry" thrown off his guard by the suddenness of the attack, exclaimed "Hallo", & faced about to discover, who & what addressed him. As soon as he ascertained who we were he begged permission to join us—& off we we went.

It seems the Mt Auburn party fell thro' & the hapless Henry, was left to his own resources, & was wandering in quest of adventures, when he met us by moonlight.— We had quite a pleasant walk & then returned to our cottage again. The two attendants entered also & paid us a visit— Upon finding that both Henry & Horace intended "turning in" to Mr Feltons apartment for the night— thought it would but a deed of charity to ask Horace to take possession of Edmunds apartment here— Which after some consultation was accepted. Laughed much over various oddities which had occur'd & then bade good night.—

Thursday—1st of August.— We presumed that Horace departed at peep of dawn, as he was seen no more.— After breakfast made a batch of gingerbread—which was pronounced to be very fine.— Mrs Greene was by appointment to be driven over to Roxbury by Henry Cleveland to see Mrs Williams— At 10—gentleman arrived and they drove off— Hardly had they departed when I was summoned to the parlour to see Mr Sumner, who came to give his daily report of Mr Alvord. Today it was indeed favorable, & there is now every hope of his being restored.—

Mr Sumner then paid me a long visit, & we talked at the rate of nine knotts an hour— Gave me a very droll account of a Mr Thomas, a young man who Mr Felton spoke of also, the other eveg—who has been studying Latin & greek, by himself, in a light house, off Barnstable, to prepare himself for College!! The reason of his choosing to reside at the lighthouse

was to save the expense of oil, as he could read by the light of the lantern!
He has now come to enter college & from all accounts we may with truth
exclaim "here comes an original"— The gentlemen say that they can only
compare him to Caspar Horsa—so entirely does he appear to be new to
the world. We were so agreeable, that Mr Sumner, remained until Mama
returned from Dedham—& finished his visit to her. Mama left Abby at D.
& found Aunt better.—

Mama then went in to see Mrs Alvord— I wrote &c Mama returned—
did not see Mrs A. as she had gone to town, for the Dr did not wish her to
be with her son as it excited him so much, & if she was in the house, he
would not be easy without her. Mrs Curtis, who has been indeed a mother
to him, never leaving him night nor day—is now quite easy about him &
thinks he will now recover.— Margaret & Henry, returned about two
o'clk—& Henry dined here— In the afternoon Aunt Jackson came out,
bringing with her, Mr & Mrs Randall of Phila Son of Sophias old admirer
& Mr R. regretted extremely her absence—as he could not see "his
belle".— Paid a short visit & departed for Mt. Auburn—where we indeed
consign all our friends—being a bourne which no traveller returns without seeing.—

Eveg. Edmund came out—& a few moments after Mrs Curtis & Mrs
Alvord came in.— Mrs A. had decided to return early the next morng. as
she found her son out of danger, & could do no good here.— She is quite
an interesting woman, but the very *image* of her Son— She expressed the
greatest gratitude for all that had been done, & felt for him by his Cambridge friends, & I shall not soon forget the tone in which, when Mama
said "She hoped that this illness would not leave an unpleasant impression upon Mr Alvord's recollections of Cambridge"— She said—"He
would indeed be an ungrateful wretch if he felt any thing but the deepest
gratitude & affection for Cambridge". She seemed to have much feeling &
I should think from all accounts was a fine woman.—

Mrs Curtis, who has been devoted to Mr Alvord, declared that she felt
now perfectly happy, and that the feeling of relief from anxiety, she considered to be the most delightful sensation in the world— Mrs C. really
seems to live for other people—& "verily she has her reward"[13]— They
paid us a short visit, & departed with every good wish, & kind invitation
exchanged—

Mr Alvord is to follow his Mother to Northfield as soon as he is able to
ride— Little did we imagine Sophy, when you wrote that note describing

Mr A's last visit, & thought it "unnecessary to wish him *health*," how much we should really *suffer* on his account, before he left Cambridge—& may now indeed wish him a return of "health", as well as "happiness."

Friday 2d— Soon after breakfast, Mama Margy & I drove to town, on purpose to go *sight seeing*. Drove first to Corinthian Hall, to see some copies of Canova's statues which Mr Felton a few evenings before had entreated us to go & see, declaring they were the most exquiste things ever beheld, & that we "seldom saw so much of the Grecian"[14]— As we presumed that we seldom saw so much of something beside the Grecian, we hesitated, as to the propriety of going—but curiosity prevailed—& we drew up to the door— Mama & Margy went up first, & said if there was nothing there to shock my tender mind, they would send down for me— So in a few moments, I was summoned. And truly they are exquiste indeed—but cannot describe— The Hebe is rather my favorite— The Graces, are *grace* indeed, & their beauty made me glad—& their having a few fluttering shades of drapery still gladder— All the specimins, are superior to anything of the kind we have seen— They have been executed in marble, by Canova's pupils.—

From thence, we walked to the Athenaeum, stopping in our way, to visit the tomb of Scipio, in Cunningham's auction room!— "To what base uses we may come at last"— (Shakespeare)[15]— Athenaeum full of strangers no one we knew— Mama made an acquaintance by accident, with a gentleman & lady from N. Y. found they were Mr & Mrs Griffin— intimate friends of Mr Omstead, the gentleman, Susan mentions in her letters— Mr G. & indeed all the party, which included a Miss Provost, & little Miss Griffin—very odd people— at first could not tell what to make of them— Both the ladies seemed excessively dull—& did not take the least interest in any thing— Mr Griffin very stiff & formal in his manners— Mama however took them under her wing carried the gentleman in to the Athenaeum &c &c—and asked them to come out to Cambridge in the P.M. & go to Mt Auburn &c which they accepted.

We then bade them good morning, & drove to the next *sight*, which is a model of a cotton manufactory—from the very begining—to the cloth woven—the whole set in motion by one great wheel, which is worked by three *dogs*, exactly on the principle of the treadmill. It is a most ingenious, & curious thing & gives you a clearer idea of the whole process than visiting fifty great cotton manufactuaries. The dogs looked contented, & we were happy to observe for their sakes, that the man had a most excellent countenance who showed it.— From there called upon Cousin Susan, & then drove to our *last* sight, which was the group of "Tam O'Shanter" & the landlord, landlady & "Souter Johnny" from Burns' poem.[16] It is executed in soft sandstone, by a self taught artist, & most admirably done— Figures as large as life, with the most admirable expression— Perfectly wonderful— They have exactly the effect of people turned into *stone*—just as they were sitting—and Burns himself would be satisfied if he could see them.— After staying there a long time, we at length drove to Cambridge, after passing a very pleasant morning.—

Afternoon rested until 4 o'ck—when Mr & Mrs Sam Hubbard are announced— They however paid but short visit— Soon after the Griffin Party arrive, & are soon wafted away by Mama & Margy, to the Library &c &c—. My solitude was enlivened by a visit from Abby Phillips & a letter from Mrs Levy.— On the return of the party, the ladies seemed much woke up—& expressed much pleasure & gratitude— From all accounts Mrs Griffin & Miss Provost have met with so many misfortunes as entirely explains their melancholy appearance—and Mr G. told Mama that he had hardly ever known them come out of themselves so much as this afternoon, & thanked her over & over—for giving them so much pleasure.— Margys account of the afternoon I shall not soon forget & all the oddities that occur'd. On taking leave, Mrs Griffin *kissed* us, and all expressed their gratitude & exchanged the usual good wishes & invitations—

In the eveg. Edmund came out—& Judge Story & Mr Greenleaf—the new Law Professor came. Mr Greenleaf very pleasing— Gentlemanly in his manners, & agreeable in his conversation a pleasing but penetrating eye, & a soft toned voice— Altogether just what we were told he was— and thats more than can be said of every body—and will I should think, be a popular Professor, & "a very agreeable addition to the *Society of Cambridge*".— Mrs Greenleaf also in Cambridge—but not yet settled.—

Saturday 3d— Morning, Mama, Margy & I went to Brookline, left M at Mrs Greenes & drove to Col Perkins'— Paid Mrs P. a long visit—went all over their place &c— Then went to Mrs Guilds, where Margy joined us— & after a visit to her returned home. Forget what we did the rest of the day.—

Sunday 4th. Staid at home all day— The rest of the family were enlightened by Mr *Johnson's* eloquence. Thunderstorm in the afternoon— Mr Wells & Fanny came— Horace Cleveland drank tea here— Mr Rutledge Mr Sumner, & Mr Felton, the eveg visitors.—

Monday 5— raining day.— Mr Appleton called—& also Mrs Guild & Elisabeth— Cleared up towards eveng. After tea, Mama Margy & I, went up to Mrs Wells—paid them a long visit, very pleasant one. On our return called on Mrs Story— Saw her & Judge Story—& Mrs Pierce, Senr, who is staying there.— At home, we found Edmund, who had been enlivened by a visit from Dr Ware.—

Tuesday 6th. Morning— Went to town—first shopped, & then paid a long visit to Martha.— Afternoon Mrs Dr Higginson came. [than?] Mrs. Phillips & Miss Johnson.— Just as we were sitting down to tea—heard the front door open—& on going in to the parlour found Tom Davis, & two other forms—one of whom he introduced as "Mr Blant a former acquaintance of yrs. Anna" & the other as Mr Harrison of Louisana— Mr Blant was enchanted to *see* me again— (Mem—the room was dark as midnight)— I could not say I was glad *hear* him again—for he *proses worser* & worser— Mr Harrison, I did not think much of at first—as he is short—& nothing remarkable in his appearance but no sooner did he take his seat beside me, & begin *really* to converse, than I soon found he was something better than the handsome Blant. With the manners of a man of the world he combined much fluency of speech, and sense, ease, which mark security to please— Altogether something quite out of the common way— Was surprised to find he intended taking up his abode for a month or two in *Cambridge*, until he could return to N. Orleans— From Tom we learned that Mr H had been in Cambridge some years since—was thought something remarkable then, & had since taken a high rank at the bar— The library & the Law school here, were his attractions to pass away the time until he could return home— Will be certainly a new character among the many already gathered under the wing of the University—a contrast certainly to the *Light house man*—

Mr Gardner entered before the other gentlemen departed— After they were gone, Mr G. sang one or two songs delightfully— but he is the oddest mortal I ever desire to entertain, & we as usual came to the satisfactory conclusion, that we can not comprehend him.—

Wednesday 7th. Morning—Mama & Edmund departed for Harvard— After they were gone, Margy & I raised the Janitor, & went over to the Library— Where we locked *ourselves in*, and passed some time "amid ages past"[17]— At lenght, steps were heard, & a knock alarmed us— I opened the door as if I expected to see a hundred lions, & lo! *Josiah*, walked in— They had reached home last eveg & had come over to see us— After an affectionate meeting ajourned home. Josiah soon left us— Passed the morning, reading & writing—*talking!* No one came *save* a deaf & dumb man, to whom Miranda *screamed* at the pitch of her voice that "*all were gone*".—

Afternoon Henry Parker came, & while I was entertaining him—Mr Robert Storer, entered— We had just began our usual flow of soul, when Abby Phillips enters the front door—but seeing a gentleman here in the parlour—cuts into the opposite room. I followed—but she would not remain as she was fearful I supposc of interrupting a tête à tête—consequently vanished. Scarcely had I again returned to Mr Storer, when Margy enters, her wild eyes flying round in search of Abby Phillips who, as she said afterwards, she had come down to take off my hands— Perceiving no trace of her, she after satisfying herself that she had not sunk into the earth—joined Henry. Mr Storer was agreable as usual—& we conversed on various topics, till a walk was proposed & accordingly, Margy & I, sallied forth, attended by Mr Storer—leaving Henry to his own reflections—

We proceeded to the Botanic Garden, & had it not been that we had the powerful arm of Mr Storer to protect us, our retreat would have been made quick step, for the cows were *carrying* on, in a manner not to be trifled with— As it was, it required all our philosophy, & all our *vanity* to pass *one* which was actually tearing the earth with her *claws*, & horns, tail & legs flying—

Mr Storer, who *had* probably been in more danger in his life—was supernaturally insensible, & seemed actually & *cruelly amused* with our terrors— We however reached the garden in safety, which looked delightfully. The evening was really exquiste, clouds, flowers trees, & distant views all quite perfect— After walking sometime in the garden, we again set forth down the haunted lane. The cows was seen cantering & curvetting before us—& various carriages flirting backwards & forwards— we therefore took a cut to the Common, & returned thro' the college yard— Had a very pleasant walk—Mr Storer, & Mrs Greene saying many smart things between them—

We had walked so slow that we did not reach home until nearly eight o'ck. & found the hapless Henry still here. Tea was immediately *served*, & Henry after forcing down a couple of mouthfuls, in evident haste & dismay—immediately took his flight—& we afterwards found that he was in great terror lest a *thunderstorm* should arise, (which to be sure existed wholly in his imagination) before he reached home.— We had an agree-able & social tea, after which Mr Storer departed.—

Thursday 8th I attempted again to be *Cousinly* & called on Abby Phillips, but she was gone to town— Margy & I then walked to Mrs Dr. Higginsons—but she was also out.— Afternoon—came Mrs & Miss Pick-ering—& after them, Mrs Williams & a Mr Davis.— Mrs Williams as lady-like, & interesting as ever, and much more cheerful, than when I last saw her. Mr Davis, was as Margy stiled him—a counter jumper— Paid but a short visit— Horace Cleveland came out to tea & Mama & Edmund re-turned in the eveg seeming to have enjoyed their jaunt very much.—

Friday 9th Made cake—recd Susans letter from Avon.— Rained all the morng—drew—& read loud in Mr Edgeworths life—which is one of the most fascinating books I ever read.[18]— Afternoon ditto—

Evening Mr Harrison came in— Had a better view of him—as I cannot say I saw him in the other evening— No personal advantages—figure not at all good—features ordinary—except a fine set of teeth, and an eye which is very expressive—evidently *one* which sees *every thing*—& at times too [piercing] observing to be agreeable— Every tone of his voice every gesture, every expression evidently studied— Conversed agreeably & fluently on various topics— Too well bred to be conceited—but perfectly *self* possessed—

One thing only struck me as not consistent— He *observed* too *obviously*—which is always a mistake, as it makes yr companion instantly suspicious—& consequently unnatural, & I am surprised that Mr Harri-son had not learnt the art of seeing without appearing to see.— He has however something about him, which immediately strikes you as uncom-mon— I cannot say he is to me wholly agreeable, as there is in him man-ners which makes me feel *uncertain* of my own ground—

Talked much of Europe Very sensible observations, and much enter-taining knowledge— Described Scenery very well— Said however that he thought a tour to Europe was a very doubtful good for a young man <*a dozen or so words crossed out*> "a visit to Europe, Miss Quincy changes the views, opinions & feelings of a young man so entirely—that on his return he can hardly be considered as the same person" <*six lines cut out*> Paid quite a long visit—& then vanished—

Saturday 10th fine day— Morning Mama departed for Quincy & Ded-ham. Margy & I walked—called on Ms Greenleaf—not at home— Mrs

Hill—saw Mrs & Miss Hill—then to call on Miss Garesché—not at home.— On our return found Mr Blounts P.P.C. on the table—but were informed by Betsy that "the gentleman said he would call again"— In a few moments a loud ring at the door— & Betsy rushing upstairs exclaims—"*he's come!*"

Supposing, I presume that Mr Blount must be some interesting or *interested* swain, I desended, & found the youth in the parlour, who met me with his usual subdued sweetness— Being arrayed in the deepest mourning, I supposed he <*six lines cut out*> common, between the two gentleman I despatched a message for Margy who came to my assistance— Mr Bartlett however soon departed—not so Mr Blount, who continued prosing on for a long time & would have remained I believe to this hour—had not another peal at the door bell aroused him— He arose, & looking more melancholy & gentlemanlike every moment made us a parting address, pressed a hand of each, said "farewell" and vanished—

Scarsely had the tall & finely formed—fairly cleared the threshold, and e'er we could drop a tear to his memory—Mr & Mrs Angier, walked into the apartment. Mr A. looked very handsome—both quite pleasing— Afternoon read &c Miss Revere & Miss Robbins came. Helen looked pretty—very pretty manners. Just as we were talking, in walked Wm. Swett—acted as odd as ever—turned to Miss Revere & asked her "how long she had been in Cambridge", was only answered by the Lady going off in an uncontroulable fit of laughter. Thought it rather odd— Soon after the ladies took leave—& at the door—Helen told me that she had been driven by Wm. Swett to Mt Auburn that afternoon, & it was his absurdity in asking her immediately after how long she had been here—that amused her so much—

Returned to the parlour where Mr Swett continued to talk in his usual distracted manner & fly from subject to subject—with frightful rapidity— Said some very good things, however. Conversation turned upon the various characters we saw in Camb. & the amusement it was to observe the difference of characters— "Yes" said I, "almost every visitor is a complete contrast to the preceeding"— "Ladies I congratulate you"—said Mr S. rising— "Your next visitor will I hope be a complete contrast to yr last"—& vanished. The extreme oddity of his manner entirely deprived us of all power of answering & as soon as he was gone, we fell back, & laughed heartily.— No visitor succeeded however—but we compared him with Mr

Blount, our morng visitor, & truly a greater contrast in appearance, manner, & conversation can hardly be imagined.—

Sunday 11th Delightful day— Morning, Margy & I attended church— Mr Newell preached for the first time for six months—very interesting services indeed. Afternoon, Mr Henry Ware—admirable as usual uncommonly animated—& impressive.— After our return Horace Cleveland came—staid to tea— After his departure, Mr Felton came paid a visit of two hours—so we will hope it was agreeable—

Monday 12. Soon after breakfast, Margy & I went to the Bath— On our return found the card of an Italian Marquis[19]—& some Phila eleganté— who had brought letters only conceive how provoking— We laid them on the table however to have it known that we knew a Marquis— I had scarsely arrayed myself—when Wm. Wadsworth was announced— Had a friendly meeting, & a pleasant visit from him— Looked in better health, & seemed in better spirits then I expected— Talked of our visit to Washington &c Showed me his little watch which was my companion during that pleasant fortnight, it did indeed recall scenes at the Capital— Wm. leaves town today.— Recd letters from the party at Niagara—all highly delighted.

Soon after "Mr Whitney" is announced—desended & found the peturbed— Had a long tête à tête—was presented with Miss Caroline Whitneys cards for the 20th!!   After the Peturbed, had rushed from the apartment, wrote to the girls but was again summoned to the Saloon to see Mrs Bigelow—Miss Garesché & brother—Mrs Bigelow quite pretty— reminded me of Mrs. Alsop— Miss Garesché pretty & pleasing—Mr Garesché a tall slender french man, not remarkable— All very conversable however & quite a pleasant vis. from them. Afternoon wrote &c. Mr & Mrs R. H Gardner came.— In the eveg—Ed. came out—& Mama returned from Quincy.—

Tuesday 13— *A real dog*— Nothwithstanding that, however, Mr & Mrs Cushing, & Nancy Perkins drove up in a "Barouche landeau"[20]— All appeared very well. Both Nabob, & Nabobess simple—and as Elisa Guild would "*neat & pleasant*"— Mr C is evidently a far more easy personage since he had Mrs C. to pay morning visits with him, & really talked quite fast & looks less like a Chinese than formerly.— For a wonder Edmund was our only visitor either afternoon or eveg

Wednesday 14th delightful day. Morning Margy & I went to town—

Shopped and paid visits all the morning— Saw no one however but Mrs Croker of Charlston, who is an oddity. Afternoon —forget what we did— Evening Mr Felton came— quite an agreeable conversation on books &c &c—

Thursday 15— Wrote a note to Miss Gareschè asking her for the evening— every thing just arranged, when letters came in saying the Niagara party will be here in the afternoon. All up in the wind—& obliged to defer Miss Gareschè.— Wrote all the morng— Afternoon the Niagara party arrived—all appearing to have enjoyed their excursion extremely— and all talking describing &c &c—until after tea— Mr Greene quite ill— In the eveg Mr Harrison, hat in hand, & dressed for conquest, tript in to the apartment— (He literally *tript* into the house for we heard a loud tumble over the board which at present ornaments our front door, & strongly opine, that the man of elegance received a most unsentimental knock.)—

As usual Mr H. & myself sat at the centre table while Mama kept up a ground swell of conversation, on the Sopha—but not on *carpets* as on a former occasion— Mr Harrison was very entertaining, but he is an artificial—heartless animal— He has however much talent—& possessing "no personal advantages," has made the most of his gift of mind & *tongue*—

Friday 16th Forget what we did— Josiah dined here— Mr Folsom came in the eveg—

Saturday 17th— Morng. wrote invitations to Miss Gareschè &c for the eveg— Then Mama & I went to town, to see the launch of Mr Parkers new vessel— Drove like fury as we had a strange horse in the carriage—found all had gone to South Boston, & therefore whipt after them. Arrived—at the shipyard— Mr Parker rushed to our assistance, & we scrambled along to the place, where Mrs P—Lucilla Abby Margy &c &c were standing— Ship nearly ready—many people looking on—scene beautiful— At last "the Baron Humbolt" passed most gracefully into her clement, amid the Hurra's of those on board—& those on shore— it was a very fine launch—& all went off very well—

We then returned to Mr Parkers & paid them a short visit & returned to Cambridge. Our Gareschè party in the eveg went off very well— Miss Davis & Mr Gardner sang delightfully— Mrs Bigelow & Miss Gareschè played admirably & are quite pleasuring— Talked a long time to Wickliffe who is a fine looking young man—& what is more has a really fine & high

character— Our list of beaux, was rather small—as every one was out of
~~Un~~ Cambridge[21]—but we passed an agreeable eveg not withstanding.—

Sunday 18th— did not go to church. Mr Wells dined here— Intended
to have gone to church in the afternoon but never woke up in time.— Edmund & Horace Cleveland drank tea here.— Mr Sparks, Mr & Mrs Higginson & Miss Storrow & Mr Campbell were the eveg visitors—

Talked to Mr Campbell who has just returned from Saratoga—& was
quite agreeable. Gave me a very amusing accounts of the various lions at
the Springs—the greatest of which at this moment is a Mr Trelawney,
who is said to be the original of Byron's *Corsair*[22]— It is *said* that he is the
younger son of a Scottish nobleman, who turned first a priveteer & met
with a variety of adventures, *married a beautiful indian girl*—who accompanied him on various of his honorable expeditions, until one day when as
she was *bathing, a shark* happened unluckily, to swallow the unhappy
demoiselle— Upon which Mr Trelawney became so distracted with rage,
grief & *Sharkentrophy* that he turned *Pirate* forthwith, and after years of adventures too numerous to mention, he returned with a broken heart & a
large fortune to England. Became acquainted with Byron, who was so
captivated by his story that he forthwith wrote the Corsair—upon it—only
giving Medora a more picturesque fate than befel the hapless Indian
beauty— The *marriage* & the *Shark*, are two points in the story that some
what shake my credulity.   Mr Trelawney—has now wandered over to
America, to seek that peace, which he certainly does not merit—and
when Mr. Campbell saw him last week, was endeavouring to forget for a
moment, the Shark & the Indian beauty—in a desperate flirtation with
Mary Livingston, at Congress Hall—but doubtless—"*the heart, the heart* is
lovely still."

All the Ladies are quite frantic of course about this gallant Rover—
Who by the by—can be no chicken if he went thro all these adventures—
Shark, and all, before the Corsair was written— However, all lines in his
face, & even a few grey hairs, may be attributed to his "life of stunt &
strife," and all the agony of mind he must have endured—& doubtless the
American ladies will go the whole Shark & even the whole pirate—to attract the admiration of Mr Trelawney.— Mr Campbell was quite entertaining & is very easy & gentlemanly.— He told me that Miss Coggswells
engagement is true &c &c. Passed quite an agreeable evening.—

Monday 19th Morning—Margy & I walked to the Botanic Garden—

had a very pleasant walk— During the morng—Mr Harrison called, to apologise for his non-appearance on Saturday evening— Paid a long visit but did not seem as much inclined to converse as usual apparently more inclined to leave the greatest part of the conversation to me—no easy matter—even in a fashionably darkened apartment—during a morng visit, with such an observer & critic as Mr Harrison.— Talked about Mr Randolph among other things— I said that I really felt disappointed when I heard of his death as I always had a great wish to see him[23]— "You would have been charmed with him" said Mr H—"for though a lion to man—he was almost a slave to woman— he had towards them truly chivalric gallantry— I never shall forget the tone in which he spoke in one of his public speeches of woman—and quoted with regard to them this line—'the smile, to which a world is weak.'" "Some of us"—continued Mr H—"who read poetry *then* were quite uncertain where that line came from & what particular smile it celebrated— Sometime afterwards I met with one very similar in Moores 'Anacrenon' from which I think Mr Randolph must have taken it"[24]— Whereupon Mr H repeated several stanzas which I had never heard before—In Moores most flattering & elegant strain—but tho' I am a *woman* & though Mr Harrison repeated them in the most soft and finished tone of voice—I regret to state they have all faded from my recollection.

Mr H ~~either is or affects to be quite sated with the~~—is a sort of man one likes to see as a sample of his species—but for all trust, & truth—give me—something more natural—something that has at least an *apology* for a heart— I shall not soon forget the tone in which he said to me the other eveg— "I was quite shocked today—Miss Q. I saw in the newspaper the notice of my friend, Mr ———'s death killed in a duel a few days since in New Orleans— He was really a elegant creature—& uncommonly gifted—but he was shot thro' the forehead—killed instantly—& what is peculiar—his opponent was one of his *most* intimate friends"— This was spoken in the coldest—most heartless manner—yet in his peculiar low voice, which seemed to render his words still more unfeeling.— I expressed some surpise at the *last* clause— "Ah" said he—"it is very dangerous to remain in New Orleans during the sickly season— We are always sure to get into a quarrel with some of our friends—which generally ends in one of the party being shot— Death is so common in New Orleans that life is scarsely regarded"— <about four lines cut out>

After Mr Harrisons departure—came a party of strangers from S.C. Mr & Mrs Webb—Miss Webb—& Mr Johnson—accompanied by Miss Shattuck & Mr Bancroft— Talked to Mr Johnson—very gentlemanly young man.— Afternoon Mrs Pierce— Evening—Horace & Henry Cleveland—& Mr Felton— Felt horridly stupid & remember nothing worth mentioning—

Tuesday 20th Morning Abby & I went to town to pay visits—with a visiting list as long as my arm— Left a pack of cards on a pack of strangers at the Tremont— Saw no one however but Miss Woolsey, who is quite pleasing—& E Grant who poor child is laid up with a sprained ankle.— Came home to dinner more dead than alive. Afternoon came the Italian Marquis, & a Russian but did not see them— Eveng, Sophia & I went to Mrs Fays to meet Miss Garesché & very few people there. <*about four lines cut out*>

Wednesday 21st Morning—forget what we did. Mary Jane & Josy dined here— In the afternoon Mrs Miller came— I went into town to go to a party at Mrs Harry Otis'— Went with Lucilla & Edmund.— A stranger party almost entirely quite amusing—various tall men with whiskers introduced, whose names, & whose [fames] have alike passed—from my recollection— Talked to Mr Walsh who introduced Miss Anna Sargeant, of Phil. who is quite pretty— Then talked to Tom Dwight—who had made his reappearance— Took seats on the Divan—

Mrs Otis introduced an odd looking man to me whose name was [Pruce] or Payne— Mr Harrison at this moment came up—regretted extremely that he had not come into town behind me that eveg that he might have received the *dust of my carriage!* "Oh the Sarpent"— Had much amusement with Mr H, & Mr Payne— Jo Williams of Baltimore, then came—looked just as he used to do—and rather better— Lothrop Motely also reappeared—& looked extremely handsome, but was not any less affected— Just come home—and just going back to Germany— Passed quite an amusing eveg— Staid in town with Lucilla.—

Thursday 22d. Immediately after breakfast Lucilla & I went down in town, met Mr Robert Storer, who walked a short distance with us & asked us whether we were *marketing*. The good gentleman we think must have been some what bewildered in mind—and meant *shopping*. Went up to Mr Hubbards to see Louisa G— She seemed—pretty well—& in better spirits. Then went in to Marthas— Saw Miss Woolsey—Martha & Mrs Salisbury—had a very pleasant visit to them. Called on E Grant—& then to Lucillas— Sat up in her room, & talked about her wedding—to take place, about the 10th of Oct. Came out of town to dinner.

Afternoon—was in the midst of a discription of Mrs Otis to Margy & Sophia & was just describing my talk with Mr Payne—& Mr Harrison & dwelling particularly on Mr Payne—when a ring at the door is heard, & word is brought up that "Mr Payne" is downstairs— And sure enough, there was the very man I was talking of— Mr Payne was accompanied by Mr Preble. "A naval gentleman" is Mr Payne, I should imagine—not particularly *handsome* but a clever sort of an animal. Paid quite an agreeable visit.— After their departure came Miss Salisbury—Miss Woolsey & young Salisbury.—

Friday 23d— Rainy day— Read Evelina.— Mr Felton & Mr Greene[25] (grandson of Genl. Greene) who was introduced to me the other eveg at Mrs Otis. Quite a clever youth. Afternoon cleaned. Evening Sophia & I went in to a party at Mrs G. Lee's for Miss Garesché— Arrived quite early—house looked very handsome—every thing very elegant.[26]— Was introduced to a Mrs Urquhart—a German lady—very pleasing, talked to her a long time—meantime rooms filling— All the strangers there Mr Harrison among the rest He soon beamed up. "Was much *chagrined*" that he had not been able to be in Cambridge for the last two days.— Talked some time & then introduced him to Mrs Urquhart and to it they went talking German— Had a few words with Robert Hooper—very ordinary—

Mr Begelow then introduced— Very handsome— I though of his "*manners by moonlight*"—but he now appears like the innocent flower.— Mrs Grant introduced the Marquis of Torrigiani—a very pleasing Italian young—interesting intelligent, & unaffected. Speaks English extremely well and is altogether the most pleasing foreigner I have seen <*page damaged*> Mrs Harry Otis sang—or rather *screamed*— Passed a very pleasant evening— Mr Fessenden armed me out—it really rolled back departed hours— Had a delightful drive home by moonlight.—

Saturday 24— delightful day— Walked & went to the bath. Mama & Susan went to Dedham— Mrs Sergeant the three Miss Sargeants— Miss Sumner & Mr Coffin called— The Philadelphians elegantly attired & quite pleasing— Mrs S. almost a Mrs Falconer. Papa went up with them to Mt Auburn.— Ben Welles next happened in, & was as dangerously fascinating as usual.— Jo Williams called—"as bright as ever"—in a short green

Etching of Anna C. L. Waterston. The only surviving likeness of Anna Quincy was made in her middle age, when she was known as Anna C. L. Waterston. From THE ARTICULATE SISTERS, edited by Mark DeWolfe Howe.

coat light underdress—& little stick— We talked at the rate of nine knotts an hour, having the events of three years to discuss. I think the little youth has improved since last we met— Poor Mr Kerr is kept at home by his tyrant father—so we shall not see his "Wee bit mouth" this summer— Afternoon Edmund & Lucilla called.— Eveg Margy & I walked in the garden. Margy wondered where she should be a year from that time— "August 24 1834"— Told her I would write it down in my journal, and remember to note it next year[27]—

APPENDIXES

A. Letter to Eliza Susan Quincy

[*Boston, c. 1852*]
Monday

Dear Susan

I am quite excited at the idea of the Austen letter which Papa has described,—not exactly in the style of Miss Bates,—but still the *fact*, that you have received a letter from the Admiral[1] & have actually in your possession one written by the very hand to which we owe so much, quite carries me off my feet! —

Mrs Jenning's delight at the idea of Col. Brandon's marrying Elinor is nothing to it! I can hardly resist rushing up *instanter* to behold them, and nothing but being obliged to remain at home this evening prevents me.— Dear Admiral Austen I think he must have been like Capt Wentworth,[2] when he was young, and just like what Capt Wentworth would be at this age.— He has replied with true naval promptness, and evidently deserves to be Miss Austens brother. Robert desires to add his sincere congratulations and thinks you most fortunate in such an autograph.— I never expected we should get so near Miss Austen in this world, tho' I have always hoped to find some "little coterie in Heaven" where I might catch a glimpse of her.—

I have had a nice visit from Papa.—

with love to all and congratulations to all true lovers of Miss Austen

I am ever thine Anna. —

If the house catches on fire tonight,—please save the letter— I cannot die without the sight.[3]

Autograph letter, *Quincy Papers*, reel 52, Massachusetts Historical Society

1. Admiral Francis W. Austen (1774–1865), Jane Austen's brother, had recently sent Susan Quincy an Austen letter. In *Emma*, Jane Austen characterizes Miss Bates as a scatterbrained woman known for her rambling discourse.

2. As readers of *Sense and Sensibility* know, the heroine Elinor does not marry the dashing Colonel Brandon. In chapter 4 of volume 3, however, Elinor's friend Mrs. Jennings mistakenly concludes that the colonel has proposed to Elinor. Captain Frederick Wentworth, a naval hero, is in love with Anne Elliot in Austen's *Persuasion*.

3. Susan Quincy subsequently forwarded a copy of this reply to the admiral. The Waterstons visited him at his home near Portsmouth, England, in June 1856 (Susan Quincy to Francis W. Austen, 22 April 1856, *Quincy Papers*, reel 54).

71 Chester Square [*Boston*]
Wednesday. [*December?* 1862]

Dear Mr Fields[1]—

I was much obliged to you for your kind note, expressive of yr satisfaction with the article on Jane Austen. Mr Waterston told me of his conversation with you Yesterday,—and I write this line to say, that I hope you will choose whatever time is best for yr own purposes, for the printing of the article— Were I entering the lists, as a magasine writer, then indeed should I have watched for the proof—but as I wrote at your request, & out of love for Miss Austen—and my dear Mrs Fields,[2] the case is quite different, and you must decide upon the whole matter. As to my name, it is hardly of consequence enough to be any mystery— I have never had any ambition to see it in print, except on my visiting card—(and now alas—I am Mrs *Waterston* placed in the front rank of age, by the vanishing away of one very dear)[3]— Still—this matter too I leave to your judgement and good taste, when ever the time comes.

with love to Mrs. Fields

I am truly yrs— Anna C. L. Waterston

Autograph letter, Huntington Library, San Marino.

1. James T. Fields (1817–81), author and publisher, had become the editor of the *Atlantic Monthly* in 1861.

2. Annie Adams Fields (1834–1915), who had married James T. Fields in 1854, was known for her literary and civic activities in Boston.

3. Robert Waterston's mother, Hepsea Lord Waterston, had apparently died recently.

Mrs. R. C. Waterston, *Atlantic Monthly* 11 (February 1863): 235–240

In the old Cathedral of Winchester stand the tombs of kings, with dates stretching back to William Rufus and Canute; here too, are the marble effigies of queens and noble ladies, of crusaders and warriors, of priests and bishops. But our pilgrimage led us to a slab of black marble set into the pavement of the north aisle, and there, under the grand old arches, we read the name of Jane Austen. Many-colored as the light which streams through painted windows, came the memories which floated in our soul as we read the simple inscription: happy hours, gladdened by her genius, weary hours, soothed by her touch; the honored and the wise who first placed her volumes in our hand; the beloved ones who had lingered over her pages, the voices of our distant home associated with every familiar story.

The personal history of Jane Austen belongs to the close of the last and the beginning of the present century. Her father through forty years was rector of a parish in the South of England. Mr. Austen was a man of great taste in all literary matters; from him his daughter inherited many of her gifts. He probably guided her early education and influenced the direction of her genius. Her life was passed chiefly in the country. Bath, then a fashionable watering-place, with occasional glimpses of London, must have afforded all the intercourse which she held with what is called "the world." Her travels were limited to excursions in the vicinity of her father's residence. Those were the days of post-chaises and sedan-chairs, when the rush of the locomotive was unknown. Steam, that genie of the vapor, was yet a little household elf, singing pleasant tunes by the evening fire, at quiet hearthstones, it has since expanded into a mighty giant, whose influences are no longer domestic. The circles of fashion are changed also. Those were the days of country-dances and India muslins; the beaux and belles of "the upper rooms" at Bath knew not the whirl of the waltz, nor the ceaseless involvements of "the German." Yet the measures of love and jealousy, of hope and fear, to which their hearts beat time, would be recognized to-night in every ballroom. Infinite sameness, infinite variety, are not more apparent in the outward than in the inward world, and the work of that writer will alone be lasting who recognizes and embodies this eternal law of the great Author.

Jane Austen possessed in a remarkable degree this rare intuition. The following passage is found in Sir Walter Scott's journal, under the date of the fourteenth of March, 1826:— "Read again, and for the third time at least, Miss Austen's finely written novel of 'Pride and Prejudice.' That young lady had a talent for describing the involvements and feelings and characters of ordinary life, which is to me the most wonderful I ever met with. The Big Bow-wow strain I can do myself like any now going, but the exquisite touch which renders ordinary commonplace things and characters interesting from truth of the description and the sentiment is denied to me." This is high praise, but it is something more when we recur to the time at which Sir Walter writes his paragraph. It is amid the dreary entries in his journal of 1826, many of which make our hearts ache and our eyes overflow. He read the pages of Jane Austen on the fourteenth of March, and on the fifteenth he writes, "This morning I leave 39 Castle Street for the last time." It was something to have written a book sought for by him at such a moment. Even at Malta, in December, 1831, when the pressure of disease, as well as of misfortune, was upon him, Sir Walter was often found with a volume of Miss Austen in his hand, and said to a friend, "There is a finishing-off in some of her scenes that is really quite above everybody else."

Jane Austen's life-world presented such a limited experience that it is marvellous where she could have found the models from which she studied such a variety of forms. It is only another proof that the secret lies in the genius which seizes, not in the material which is seized. We have been told by one who knew her well, that Miss Austen never intentionally drew portraits from individuals, and avoided, if possible, all sketches that could be recognized. But she was so faithful to Nature, that many of her acquaintance, whose characters had never entered her mind, were much offended, and could not be persuaded that they or their friends had not been depicted in some of her less attractive personages: a feeling which we have frequently shared; for, as the touches of her pencil brought out the light and shades very quietly, we have been startled to recognize our own portrait come gradually out on the canvas, especially since we are not equal to the courage of Cromwell, who said, "Paint me as I am."

In the "Autobiography of Sir Egerton Brydges" we find the following passage: it is characteristic of the man: —

"I remember Jane Austen, the novelist, a little child. Her mother was a Miss Leigh, whose paternal grandmother was a sister of the first Duke of Chandos. Mr. Austen was of a Kentish family, of which several branches have been settled in the Weald, and some are still remaining there. When I knew Jane Austen, I never suspected she was an authoress; but my eyes told me that she was fair and handsome, slight and elegant, with cheeks a little too full. The last time, I think, I saw her was at Ramsgate, in 1803; perhaps she was then about twenty-seven years old. Even then I did not know that she was addicted to literary composition."

We can readily suppose that the spheres of Jane Austen and Sir Egerton could not be very congenial; and it does not appear that he was ever tempted from the contemplation of his own performances, to read her "literary compositions." A letter from Robert Southey to Sir Egerton shows that the latter had not quite forgotten her. Southey writes, under the date of Keswick, April, 1830:—

"You mention Miss Austen; her novels are more true to Nature, and have (for my sympathies) passages of finer feeling than any others of this age. She was a person of whom I have heard so much, and think so highly, that I regret not having seen her, or ever had an opportunity of testifying to her the respect which I felt for her."

A pleasant anecdote, told to us on good authority in England, is illustrative of Miss Austen's power over various minds. A party of distinguished literary men met at a country-seat; among them was Macaulay, and, we believe, Hallam; at all events, they were men of high reputation. While discussing the merits of various authors, it was proposed that each should write down the name of that work of fiction which had given him the greatest pleasure. Much surprise and amusement followed; for, on opening the slips of paper, *seven* bore the name of "Mansfield Park,"—a coincidence of opinion most rare, and a tribute to an author unsurpassed.

Had we been of that party at the English country-house, we should have written, "The *last* novel by Miss Austen which we have read"; yet, forced to a selection, we should have named "Persuasion." But we withdraw our private preference, and, yielding to the decision of seven wise men, place "Mansfield Park" at the head of the list, and leave it there without further comment.

"Persuasion" was her latest work, and bears the impress of a matured mind and perfected style. The language of Miss Austen is, in all her pages, drawn from the "wells of English undefiled." Concise and clear, simple and vigorous, no word can be omitted that she puts down, and none can be added to heighten the effect of her sentences. In "Persuasion" there are passages whose depth and tenderness, welling up from deep fountains of feeling, impress us with the conviction that the angel of sorrow or suffering had troubled the waters, yet had left in them a healing influence, which is felt rather than revealed. Of all the heroines we have known through a long and somewhat varied experience, there is not one whose life-companionship we should so desire to secure as that of Anne Elliot. Ah! could she also forgive our faults and bear with our weaknesses, while we were animated by her sweet and noble example, existence would be, under any aspect, a blessing. This felicity was reserved for Captain Wentworth. Happy man! In "Persuasion" we also find the subtle Mr. Elliot. Here, as with Mr. Crawford in "Mansfield Park," Miss Austen deals dexterously with the character of a man of the world, and uses a nicer discernment than is often found in the writings of women, even those who assume masculine names.

"Emma" we know to have been a favorite with the author. "I have drawn a character full of faults," said she, "nevertheless I like her." In Emma's company we meet Mr. Knightley, Harriet Smith, and Frank Churchill. We sit beside good old Mr. Woodhouse, and please him by tasting his gruel. We walk through Highbury, we are patronized by Mrs. Elton, listen forbearingly to the indefatigable Miss Bates, and take an early walk to the post-office with Jane Fairfax. Once we found ourselves actually on "Box Hill," but it did not seem half so real as when we "explored" there with the party from Highbury.

"Pride and Prejudice" is piquant in style and masterly in portraiture. We make perhaps too many disagreeable acquaintances to enjoy ourselves entirely; yet who would forego Mr. Collins, or forget Lady Catherine de Bourgh, though each in their way is more stupid and odious than any one but Miss Austen could induce us to endure. Mr. Darcy's character is ably given; a very difficult one to sustain under all the circumstances in which he is placed. It is no small tribute to the power of the author to concede that she has so managed the workings of his real nature as to make it

151

possible, and even probable, that a high-born, high-bred Englishman of Mr. Darcy's stamp could become the son-in-law of Mrs. Bennet. The scene of Darcy's declaration of love to Elizabeth, at the Hunsford Parsonage, is one of the most remarkable passages in Miss Austen's writings, and, indeed, we remember nothing equal to it among the many writers of fiction who have endeavored to describe that culminating point of human destiny.

"Northanger Abbey" is written in a fine vein of irony, called forth, in some degree, by the romantic school of Mrs. Radcliffe and her imitators. We doubt whether Miss Austen was not over-wise with regard to these romances. Though born after the Radcliffe era, we well remember shivering through the "Mysteries of Udolpho" with as quaking a heart as beat in the bosom of Catherine Morland. If Miss Austen was not equally impressed by the power of these romances, we rejoice they were written, as with them we should have lost "Northanger Abbey." For ourselves, we spent one very rainy day in the streets of Bath, looking up every nook and corner familiar in the adventures of Catherine, and time, not faith, failed, for a visit to Northanger itself. Bath was also sanctified by the presence of Anne Elliot. Our inn, the "White Hart," (made classic by the adventures of various well-remembered characters,) was hallowed by exquisite memories which connected one of the rooms (we faithfully believed it was our apartment) with the conversation of Anne Elliot and Captain Harville, as they stood by the window, while Captain Wentworth listened and wrote. In vain did we gaze at the windows of Camden Place. No Anne Elliot appeared.

"Sense and Sensibility" was the first novel published by Miss Austen. It is marked by her peculiar genius, though it may be wanting in the nicer finish which experience gave to her later writings.

The Earl of Carlisle, when Lord Morpheth, wrote a poem for some now forgotten annual, entitled "The Lady and the Novel." The following lines occur among the verses:—

> "Or is it thou, all-perfect Austen? here
> Let one poor wreath adorn thy early bier
> That scarce allowed thy modest worth to claim
> The living portion of thy honest fame:
> Oh, Mrs. Benet, Mrs. Norris, too,
> While Memory survives, she'll dream of you;
> And Mr. Woodhouse, with abstemious lip,
> Must thin, but not too thin, the gruel slip;
> Miss Bates, our idol, though the village bore,
> And Mrs. Elton, ardent to explore;
> While the clear style flows on without pretence,
> With unstained purity, and unmatched sense."

If the Earl of Carlisle, in whose veins flows "the blood of all the Howards," is willing to acknowledge so many of our friends, who are anything but aristocratic, our republican soul shrinks not from the confession that we should like to accompany good-natured Mrs. Jennings in her hospitable carriage, (so useful to our young ladies of sense and sensibility,) witness the happiness of Elinor at the parsonage, and the reward of Colonel Brandon at the manor-house of Delaford, and share with Mrs. Jennings all the charms of the mulberry-tree and the yew arbor.

An article on "Recent Novels," in "Fraser's Magazine" for December, 1847, written by Mr. G. H. Lewes, contains the following paragraphs:—"What we must heartily enjoy and applaud is truth in the delineation's of life and character. . . . To make our meaning precise, we would say that Fielding and Miss Austen are the greatest novelists in our language. . . . We would rather have written 'Pride and Prejudice,' or 'Tom Jones,' than any of the 'Waverley Novels.' . . . Miss Austen has been called a prose Shakspeare,—and among others, by Macaulay. In spite of the sense of incongruity which besets us in the words *prose* Shakspeare, we confess the greatness of Miss Austen, her marvellous dramatic power, seems, more than anything in Scott, akin to Shakspeare."

The conclusion of this article is devoted to a review of "Jane Eyre," and led to the correspondence between Miss Brontè and Mr. Lewes which will be found in the memoir of her life. In these letters it is apparent that Mr. Lewes wishes Miss Brontè to read and to enjoy Miss Austen's works, as he does himself. Mr. Lewes is disappointed, and felt, doubtless, what all true lovers of Jane Austen have experienced, a surprise to find how obtuse otherwise clever people sometimes are. In this instance, however, we think Mr. Lewes expected what was impossible. Charlotte Brontè could not harmonize with Jane Austen. The luminous and familiar star which comes forth into the quiet evening sky when the sun sets amid the amber light of an autumn evening, and the comet which started into sight, unheralded and unnamed, and flamed across the midnight sky, have no affinity, except in the Divine Mind, whence both originate.

The notice of Miss Austen, by Macaulay, to which Mr. Lewes alludes, must be, we presume, the passage which occurs in Macaulay's article on Madame D'Arblay, in the "Edinburgh Review," for January, 1843. We do not find the phrase, "prose Shakspeare," but the meaning is the same; we give the passage as it stands before us:—

"Shakspeare has neither equal nor second; but among writers who, in the point we have noticed, have approached nearest the manner of the great master, we have no hesitation in placing Jane Austen, as a woman of whom England is justly proud. She has given us a multitude of characters, all, in a certain sense, commonplace, all such as we meet every day. Yet they are all as perfectly discriminated from each other as if they were the most eccentric of human beings. There are, for example, four clergymen, none of whom we should be surprised to find in any parsonage in the kingdom,—Mr. Edward Ferrars, Mr. Henry Tilney, Mr. Edward Bertram, and Mr. Elton. They are all specimens of the upper part of the middle class. They have been all liberally educated. They all lie under the restraints of the same sacred profession. They are all young. They are all in love. Not any one of them has any hobby-horse, to use the phrase of Sterne. Not one has any ruling passion, such as we read in Pope. Who would not have expected them to be insipid likenesses of each other? No such thing. Harpagon is not more unlike Jourdain, Joseph Surface is not more unlike Sir Lucius O'Trigger, than every one of Miss Austen's young divines to all his reverend brethren. And almost all this is done by touches so delicate that they almost elude analysis, that they defy the powers of description, and that we know them to exist only by the general effect to which they have contributed."

Dr. Whately, the Archbishop of Dublin, in the "Quarterly Review," 1821, sums up his estimate of Miss Austen with these words: "The Eastern monarch who proclaimed a reward to him who should discover a new pleasure would have deserved well of mankind, had he stipulated it should be blameless. Those again who delight in the study of human nature may improve in the knowledge of it, and in the profitable application of that knowledge, by the perusal of such fictions.["] Miss Austen introduces very little of what is technically called religion into her books, yet that must be a blinded soul which does not recognize the vital essence, everywhere present in her pages, of a deep and enlightened piety.

There are but few descriptions of scenery in her novels. The figures of the piece are her care; and if she draws in a tree, a hill, or a manor-house, it is always in the background. This fact did not arise from any want of appreciation for the glories or the beauties of the outward creation, for we know that the pencil was as often in her hand as her pen. It was the unity of purpose, ever present in her mind, which never allowed her to swerve from the actual into the ideal, nor even to yield to tempting descriptions of Nature which might be near, and yet aside from the main object of her narrative. Her creations are living people, not masks behind which the author soliloquizes or lectures. These novels are impersonal; Miss Austen never herself appears; and if she ever had a lover, we cannot decide whom he resembled among the many masculine portraits she has drawn.

Very much has been said in her praise, and we, in this brief article, have summoned together witnesses to the extent of her powers, which are fit and not few. Yet we are aware that to a class of readers Miss Austen's novels must ever remain sealed books. So be it. While the English language is read, the world will always be provided with souls who can enjoy the rare excellence of that rich legacy left to them by her genius.

Once in our lifetime we spent three delicious days in the Isle of Wight, and then crossed the water to Portsmouth. After taking a turn on the ramparts in memory of Fanny Price, and looking upon the harbor whence the Thrush went out, we drove over Portsdown Hill to visit the surviving member of that household which called Jane Austen their own.

We had been preceded by a letter, introducing us to Admiral Austen as fervent admirers of his sister's genius, and were received by him with a gentle courtesy most winning to our heart.

In the finely-cut features of the brother, who retained at eighty years of age much of the early beauty of his youth, we fancied we must see a resemblance to his sister, of whom there exists no portrait.

It was delightful to us to hear him speak of "Jane," and to be brought so near the actual in her daily life. Of his sister's fame as a writer the Admiral spoke understandingly, but reservedly.

We found the old Admiral safely moored in that most delightful of havens, a quiet English country-home, with the beauty of Nature around the mansion, and the beauty of domestic love and happiness beneath its hospitable roof.

There we spent a summer day, and the passing hours seemed like the pages over which we had often lingered, written by her hand whose influence had guided us to those she loved. That day, with all its associations, has become a sacred memory, and links us to the sphere where dwells that soul whose gift of genius has rendered immortal the name of Jane Austen.

NOTES

NOTES TO THE INTRODUCTION

1. For a discussion of this trait, see Steven E. Kagle and Lorenza Gramegna, "Rewriting Her Life: Fictionalization and the Use of Fictional Models in Early American Women's Diaries," in *Inscribing the Daily: Critical Essays on Women's Diaries*, ed. Suzanne Bunkers and Cynthia Huff (Amherst: University of Massachusetts Press, 1996), 40–42, 53–55.

2. Eliza Susan Quincy, *Memoir of the Life of Eliza S. M. Quincy* (Boston: John Wilson and Son, 1861), 142, 266. The only version of Anna Quincy Waterston's autobiographical sketch (hereafter cited as Notes) is a sixty-three-page typescript in Widener Library at Harvard University. In it Anna writes that she was encouraged by a friend to compose this sketch (42). A note accompanying the typescript, to F. Lewis Gay from H. T. Otis, 17 February 1908, states that he is returning these notes by Anna Quincy Waterston. Widener Library formally accessioned this document in 1916; the quotations occur on pages 9 and 10.

3. Edward Pessen, *Riches, Class, and Power before the Civil War* (Lexington, Mass.: D. C. Heath, 1973), 331–32; Notes, 14.

4. Notes, 32–33; Pessen, *Riches, Class, and Power*, 193, 195.

5. Notes, 2, 4, 11, 38.

6. Notes, 37; Ednah Dow Cheney, "The Women of Boston," in Justin Winsor, *The Memorial History of Boston* (Boston: James R. Osgood, 1881), 4:344; Mrs. John (Eliza) Farrar, *The Young Lady's Friend* (New York: Samuel S. and William Wood, 1838), 3–5, 7; *The Young Lady's Own Book: A Manual of Intellectual Improvement and Moral Development* (Philadelphia: Key, Mielke and Biddle, 1832), 63, 71–77, 79. See also introduction to Chapter 3, below.

7. Robert A. McCaughey, *Josiah Quincy 1772–1864: The Last Federalist* (Cambridge: Harvard University Press, 1974), 124–28; E. Quincy, *Memoir*, 101; Notes, 9, 4; Marc Friedlaender and Robert Sparks, eds., *Papers Relating to the Quincy, Wendell, Holmes and Upham Families Papers* (hereafter cited as *Quincy Papers*) (Boston: Massachusetts Historical Society, 1977), reel 11.

8. Notes, 46, 47, 49.

9. Cheney, "The Women of Boston," 331–32; Notes, 9.

10. Farrar, *The Young Lady's Friend*, 220–21; Lydia Sigourney, *Letters to Young Ladies*, 2d ed. (Hartford: William Watson, 1835), 164, 179; *The Young Lady's Own Book*, 20, 190. See also John F. Kasson, *Rudeness and Civility: Manners in Nineteenth-Century Urban America* (New York: Hill and Wang, 1990), 162–63.

11. Farrar, *The Young Lady's Friend*, 375–76.

12. Edmund Quincy diary, entries for 25 February 1839 and 21 April 1840, *Quincy Papers*, reel 8; Henry Ware Jr., "Discourse Preached at the Ordination of Mr. Robert C. Waterston as Minister at Large, Nov. 24, 1839" (Boston: Isaac R. Butts, 1840).

13. Josiah P. Quincy, "Memoir of Robert Cassie Waterston," *Massachusetts Historical Society Proceedings*, 2d series, 8 (October 1893): 302.

14. Unidentified clipping, Harvard University Archives; R. C. Waterston, "Address on Pauperism" (Boston: C. C. Little and J. Brown, 1844); R. C. Waterston, "Farewell Discourses Preached at the Church in Bedford-Street, Sunday, May 2, 1852" (Boston: John Wilson and Son, 1852).

15. Beverly Wilson Palmer, ed., *Charles Sumner Papers* (Alexandria, Va.: Chadwyck-Healey, 1988), 11/378; 26/360, 488; 29/361; 67/309; Anna Quincy Waterston to Edmund Quincy, 29 August 1856, *Quincy Papers*, reel 11; Mrs. R. C. Waterston (Anna Cabot Lowell Quincy Waterston), *Verses* (Boston: J. Wilson and Son, 1863), 68–69.

16. *Quincy Papers*, reel 11; Anna Quincy Waterston to Anna Hazard Ward, 25 August 1858, Houghton Library, Harvard University.

17. *Adelaide Phillipps, a Record* (Boston: A. Williams, 1883); letters to Kate Field, Manuscript Collection, Boston Public Library.

18. Anna Quincy Waterston, "Annesley Hall and Newstead Abbey," *Atlantic Monthly* 13 (February 1864): 239–44; "The Visible and Invisible in Libraries," *Atlantic Monthly* 16 (November 1865): 525–35; "Woman's Work in the Middle Ages," *Atlantic Monthly* 18 (September 1866): 274–88. See also Anna Quincy Waterston to James T. Fields, [January? 1863], 12 June 1863, [1866?], Huntington Library, San Marino California.

19. Anna Quincy Waterston, "Woman's Work in the Middle Ages," 280–83, 285.

20. Records of Woman's Education Association, Massachusetts Historical Society.

21. Anna Quincy Waterston to Oliver Wendell Holmes, 2 September 1893, Houghton Library.

22. Notes, 63.

23. See Steven E. Kagle, *Early Nineteenth-Century American Diary Literature* (Boston: Twayne Publishers, 1986), 5–7; Lynn Z. Bloom, "'I Write for Myself and Strangers': Private Diaries as Public Documents," in Bunkers and Huff, *Inscribing the Daily*, 24, 31–32.

24. Compare, for example, Anna's entry of 21 March—"The day was lowring, chilly, dark, the roads were deep & boggy, the night was dark & foggy, & we of course did not anticipate any of 'our hens' would *peck* their way out here" with Margaret's of 8 September 1824, written when she was eighteen: "Lo! It raineth, it bloweth and it stormeth. What is to become of the Quincy party this evening?" Mark A. De Wolfe Howe, ed., *The Articulate Sisters* (Cambridge: Harvard University Press, 1946), 75.

25. Letter to Eliza Susan Quincy, *Quincy Papers*, reel 52 (see Appendix A); Anna Quincy Waterston, "Jane Austen," *Atlantic Monthly* 11 (February 1863): 235–40 (see Appendix C).

NOTES TO BIOGRAPHICAL DIRECTORY

1. Storer Family Genealogy, Massachusetts Historical Society, Boston.

2. F. Edward Wright, *Maryland Eastern Shore Vital Records, 1801–25* (Silver Spring, Md.: Family Line Publications, 1986) 5:59; F. Edward Wright, *Maryland Eastern Shore Newspaper Abstracts* (Silver Spring, Md.: Family Line Publications, 1983), 5, 102.

3. Ibid.

4. James M. and William F. Crafts, *A Genealogical and Biographical History of the Descendants of Griffin and Alice Craft* (Northampton, Mass.: Gazette Printing Co., 1893), 325.

5. William Powell, ed., *Dictionary of North Carolina Biography* (Chapel Hill: University of North Carolina Press, 1988), 3:322–23.

6. Mary I. Gozzaldi, *Supplement and Index to History of Cambridge, Mass.* (Cambridge: Cambridge Historical Society, 1930), 377.

7. Robert Lucid, ed., *Journal of Richard Henry Dana Jr.* (Cambridge: Belknap Press of Harvard University Press, 1968), 17–19.

8. *Memoir*, 255.

9. Andrew Hilen, ed., *Letters of Henry Wadsworth Longfellow* (Cambridge: Belknap Press of Harvard University Press, 1972), 4:292.

10. George T. Davis, "Biographical Sketch of Isaac P. Davis," *Massachusetts Historical Society Proceedings* 9 (July 1869): 94–96.

11. Ibid., 95.

12. CFA Diary 5:159.

13. Nathalia Wright, ed., *Letters of Horatio Greenough, American Sculptor* (Madison: University of Wisconsin Press, 1972), 45.

14. Ibid., 219–20, 251.

15. Grant Genealogy, Massachusetts Historical Society.

16. Ibid.

17. Robert C. Winthrop, "Memoir of William Minot," *Massachusetts Historical Society Proceedings* 13 (March 1874): 258.

18. Minot Family Papers, Massachusetts Historical Society.

19. New England Historic Genealogical Society, *Memorial Biographies of the New England Historic Genealogical Society* (Boston: NEHGS, 1880), 1:260.

20. Ibid.

21. Salisbury Genealogy, Massachusetts Historical Society.

22. Russell Family Genealogy, Massachusetts Historical Society.

23. Wright, ed., *Letters of Horatio Greenough*, 251; Nathalia Wright, *Horatio Greenough: The First American Sculptor* (Philadelphia: University of Pennsylvania Press, 1963), 198–99.

24. Edward Elbridge Salisbury, *Family-Memorials* (New Haven: privately printed, 1885), 73.

25. Malcolm Storer, *Annals of the Storer Family* (Boston: Wright and Potter, 1927), 53, 60–61.

NOTES TO CHAPTER 1

1. Charles Eliot Norton, "Reminiscences of Old Cambridge," *Cambridge Historical Society Publications* 1 (October 1905): 21.

2. *Catalogue of the Officers and Students of Harvard University for the Academical Year 1832–33* (Cambridge: Brown, Shattuck, and Company, 1832) (hereafter cited as *Catalogue*), 5–6, 22; Thomas Cushing, "Undergraduate Life Sixty Years Ago," *Harvard Graduates Magazine* 1 (July 1893): 549; Ronald Story, *Harvard and the Boston Upper Class* (Middletown, Conn.: Wesleyan University Press, 1980), 116.

3. *Catalogue*, 23–25; Cushing, "Undergraduate Life," 552–53.

4. *Catalogue*, 25–28, 32. Regular attendance in the law school for the non-Harvard graduates was somewhat flexible, which may explain the midterm arrival of Thomas Church on 3 April and the departure of William Chaplain a month later.

5. Norton, "Reminiscences," 19; Story, *Harvard and the Boston Upper Class*, 22; *Eighth Report of the President of Harvard University to the Overseers, 1832–33* (Cambridge: Charles Folsom, 1834), 6.

6. Story, *Harvard and the Boston Upper Class*, 45; McCaughey, *Josiah Quincy*, 168–69; Norton, "Reminiscences," 20; Seymour M. Lipset, "Political Controversies at Harvard, 1636–1974," in *Education and Politics at Harvard* (New York: McGraw-Hill, 1975), 70–71.

7. Andrew P. Peabody, *Harvard Reminiscences* (Boston: Ticknor and Company, 1888), 34; Notes, 47; Cushing, "Undergraduate Life," 559.

8. Notes, 46.

9. AQ later added: "Before Railroads!"

10. Musidora was the heroine in James Thomson's poem "Summer" (1727), from his longer work *The Seasons*.

11. Possibly *A German Prince and His Victim Taken from the Memoirs of Pauline Adelaide Alexandre Panam* (London: Sherwood, Jones, 1823).

12. The naturalist and animal painter John James Audubon (1785–1851) and his wife, Lucy Bakewell Audubon (1787–1874), having wintered in Boston, were preparing for a trip to Labrador. In Boston Audubon had been raising funds to publish additional volumes of his *Birds of America*, the first volume of which had appeared in 1830. The "Eagle" to which AQ refers was Audubon's illustration of a golden eagle from the White Mountains that he had killed in his Boston laboratory. Audubon submitted his illustration of the eagle to his engraver on 28 April; it appears as plate 181 in volume 1 of *Birds of America*. Waldemar H. Fries, *The Double Elephant Folio: The Story of Audubon's* Birds of America (Chicago: American Library Association, 1973), 70–72, 400. Mr. Channing is William Ellery Channing (1780–1842), the Unitarian theologian and brother of Harvard professor Edward T. Channing.

13. The party was at 25 Somerset Street, the home of Katherine Bigelow Lawrence. She was the wife of the textile manufacturer and merchant Abbott Lawrence.

14. John W. Audubon (1812–62) was the son of the naturalist. Samuel T. Armstrong (1784–1850) was Massachusetts lieutenant governor, 1833–35. "Aromatic vinegar" was carried in a small box in order to revive oneself when feeling faint; thus AQ describes Armstrong as quickly changing his demeanor at the approach of the Massachusetts governor, Levi Lincoln (1782–1868).

15. Here and later in this entry (with the references to Count Paris and the apothecary), the Unitarian clergyman Nathaniel L. Frothingham and AQ allude to the deadly feud in Shakespeare's *Romeo and Juliet* between the Montagues and the Capulets. Count Paris was a suitor of Juliet's; the apothecary sold Romeo the poison with which he committed suicide.

16. "Erin, the Tear and the Smile in Thine Eyes," song by Thomas Moore (1779–1852); "Come, Rest in This Bosom," also by Thomas Moore.

17. A waiter is a tray for dishes.

18. During the Roman empire, a fashionable resort.

19. In Austen's *Sense and Sensibility*, John Dashwood is the half-brother of the heroines, Elinor and Marianne Dashwood. He and his wife, Fanny, cold-heartedly evict his sisters from their family home after their father's death.

20. "Soul breathing intercourse": perhaps an adaptation from "Speed the soft intercourse from soul to soul," Alexander Pope, "Eloise to Abelard," line 57. Sir Walter Scott, "The Lay of the Last Minstrel," canto 6, stanza 1.

21. AQ later added with an X in margin "These innocent darlings now J.P. Q. & Genl. S M Q. have certainly since done their part in living and—flirting—& in fighting also, as Genl Q's record during the war shows 1869."

22. AQ calls law student William Chaplain "Leicester" apparently after Robert Dudley (1532?–88), earl of Leicester, a courtier in Queen Elizabeth's court. In *Kenilworth* (1821) Sir Walter Scott depicts him as a deceived character who is tricked into passionately ordering his wife to be killed; however, AQ may be referring to another fictional portrayal of the courtier. George Gordon, Lord Byron, "Security shall make repose more sweet," *Corsair*, canto 1, line 463.

Items making up the "shrine of Lafayette" are likely two armchairs with flag seats that Harvard apparently acquired when the Marquis de Lafayette visited in August 1824, and a print of Lafayette that Josiah Quincy purchased the same year (inventory of furniture in Wadsworth House, 17 February 1849, President's Papers, E. Everett letters, vol. 2, Harvard University Archives; inventory of furniture in Quincy household compiled by Eliza Susan Quincy, 1879, *Quincy Papers*, reel 7).

23. Probably Edward Salisbury. For the "heir apparent" see note 8 to entry for May 1, below.

24. AQ later added at the bottom of the page in pencil: "*now 1869. The Rev Francis Vinton D D— Long one of the pillars of the Episcopal Ch in NY!"

25. Conventions of the time regarded the waltz, which brings male and female bodies close together, as promiscuous. As an unmarried woman, Anna would not have been expected to waltz, although Miss Marshall did engage in this "exhibition." Etiquette book quoted in Arthur M. Schlesinger, *Learning How to Behave: A Historical Study of American Etiquette Books* (New York: Macmillan, 1947), 25. After "Sullivan" AQ later interlined, in pencil: "simple souls!!!"

26. Possibly a reference to the "Old Oaken Bucket," lyrics by Samuel Woodworth (1818), in which the narrator longs for his lost childhood.

27. John Howard Payne (1791–1852), actor, playwright, and composer of "Home Sweet Home." See also entry for April 3.

28. Louisa Gore and her mother, Mary Babcock Gore Russell, had apparently been forced by straitened circumstances to leave their home in fashionable Park Street for a simpler residence in "The Plains," that is, Jamaica Plain (see also entry for April 15). Their financial predicament must have been temporary, however, for later Louisa traveled with her mother and stepfather, Joseph Russell, to Europe. And when she married Horatio Greenough in 1837, she reportedly had an inheritance of at least $100,000 (Wright, *Horatio Greenough*, 199; Wright, ed., *Letters of Horatio Greenough*, 219, 243).

29. Adding a small penciled X here, AQ later wrote at the bottom of the page, also in pencil: "Jones died in 1856 I believe. He was a unique character, a man of uncommon talent, magnetic; but wholly devoid of truth. In appearance he was very like the portrait of Robert Burns.—"

30. The Sullivan party was probably at the home of the lawyer William Sullivan at 15 Chesnut Street.

31. AQ added later after "Morse": "died 1864."

32. Custom dictated that a woman could sit at the head of the table with other men, but should retreat when the men began their after-dinner conversation and drinking (Farrar, *The Young Lady's Friend*, 348).

33. AQ has abbreviated Cambridge to simply "C—"; hereafter the name will be silently expanded.

34. AQ has written "30th," one of her many misdatings. These mistakes have been corrected silently.

NOTES TO CHAPTER 2

1. Catherine Clinton, *Fanny Kemble's Civil Wars* (New York: Simon and Schuster, 2000), 42–43, 47, 54.

2. "The Kembles," *Boston Evening Transcript*, 24 April 1833, p. 2; *Boston Daily Advertiser*, 26 April 1833, p. 3; 30 April 1833, p. 2.

3. *Journal by Frances Anne Butler* (London: John Murray, 1835), 2:180, 206.

4. Notes, 40, 43.

5. Ibid., 43. See also Kasson, *Rudeness and Civility*, 217–22, 228–46.

6. "The Departure," *Boston Evening Transcript*, 18 May 1833, p. 2.

7. John Ashmun (b. 1799), Harvard M.A., 1818, Royall Professor of Law at Harvard University.

8. One of the earlier definitions of this word, according to the *Oxford English Dictionary*, was to circulate, move, or pass through.

9. The address of Mrs. G. H. Barrett, a frequent performer in Boston theatricals, closed with these lines: "The author, bringing forms to life and light, / which here reflected you may see to-night— / At length has come—Heaven grant no more to roam— / To his own native land, his 'home, sweet home!'" William W. Clapp Jr., *A Record of the Boston Stage* (Boston: James Munroe and Company, 1853), 303.

10. John Howard Payne's *Lancers*, a comedy first acted in New York in 1828, was one of the plays performed at this benefit, given for him by the citizens of Boston; Louisa Marston (d. 1877) may be the British actress, the wife of Henry Marston. Clapp, *A Record of the Boston Stage*, 301; George C. D. Odell, *Annals of the New York Stage* (New York: Columbia University Press 1927–49), 3:338; Westland Marston, *Our Recent Actors* (London: S. Low, Marston, Searle and Rivington, 1888), 2:56. Shakespeare, *Hamlet*, 1.5.108 (references are to act, scene, and line).

11. Howard Payne also wrote *Charles 2d* (1824), a comedy. "Thou didst drink the stale of horses," Shakespeare, *Antony and Cleopatra*, 1.4.61–62.

12. AQ had left on 5 April 1832 with Louisa Gore and her mother, Mary Babcock Gore Russell, for a tour of the South. They returned 19 May (Edmund Quincy diary, entries for 4 April and 19 May 1832, *Quincy Papers*, reel 8). Although the trio's exact itinerary is unknown, AQ mentions visiting Norfolk, the Natural Bridge in Virginia, and Washington, D.C., in her entries for 19 March, above, and for 1 May and 12 August, below.

13. A hymn by Isaac Watts.

14. Mt. Auburn in Cambridge was designed in 1831 and officially opened in 1832. AQ probably refers to a plot of land there owned by the Boston physician George C. Shattuck. Partly a cemetery and partly a park, Mt. Auburn became the repository of many celebrated Massachusetts figures, including Charles Sumner. Anna and Robert Waterston themselves would be buried there. Bainbridge Bunting and Robert H. Nylander, *Report Four: Old Cambridge* (Cambridge: MIT Press, 1973), 69–71; *Vital Records of Cambridge*. In her journal of her visit to Boston, Fanny Kemble describes a visit to Mt. Auburn on 15 April: "The enclosure is of considerable extent,—about one hundred acres,—and contains several high hills and deep ravines. . . . already two or three white monuments are seen glimmering palely through the woods, reminding one of the solemn use of which this ground is consecrated, which, for its beauty, might seem a pleasure-garden instead of a place of graves." *Journal by Frances Anne Butler*, 2: 176.

15. Jane Austen, *Persuasion* (1817).

16. Jared and Frances Sparks then occupied an apartment in the Craigie House mansion on Brattle Street, built in 1759 by John Vassall. Elizabeth Craigie regularly rented out rooms to a number of lodgers. Henry W. Longfellow Dana, "Chronicles of the Craigie House," *Cambridge Historical Society Publications* 25 (1939): 20.

17. AQ repeatedly expressed her admiration for Thomas Adams Jr. (1809–37), a lieutenant in the U.S. Army and a grandson of John Adams: "better than handsome, his character was manly, and his record worthy of the name he bore" (Notes, 28). After he was killed fighting the Indians in Florida, she wrote the poem "In Memory of a Friend, Thomas B. Adams. U.S.A.," *Verses*, 28).

18. "Et tu Brute," Shakespeare, *Julius Caesar*, 3.1.79; "men were deceivers ever," Shakespeare, *Much Ado about Nothing*, 2.3.65. "Most friendship is feigning," Shakespeare, *As You Like It*, 2.7.181; "Sir Oliver, we live in a damn'd wicked world, and the fewer we praise the better," says Sir Peter Teazle in Richard Sheridan's *School for Scandal*, 5.2.190.

19. E. K. Whitaker ran a dry goods store, specializing in French products, at 93 Washington Street.

20. "You are no better than you should be," Francis Beaumont and John Fletcher, *The Coxcomb*, 4.3.

21. "And looks a bloodless Image of Despair!" Alexander Pope, trans., *Iliad*, book 13, line 365.

22. AQ's opinion of Kemble's looks was not uncommon. Charles Francis Adams commented that he "thought her an ugly, bright looking girl," as did many others who met her (CFA *Diary* 5:74; see also Clinton, *Fanny Kemble's Civil Wars*, 41).

23. "To wipe the tears from all afflicted eyes," Pope, trans., *Odyssey*, book 17, line 14.

24. *The Stranger*, by August von Kotzebue, had been translated and adapted for the American stage by William Dunlap in 1798 (Odell, *Annals of the New York Stage*, 2:44–45). In the play, Mrs. Haller is a disguised countess who, tricked into believing her husband unfaithful, abandons her children and runs off with another man. Her husband, revealed as the "Stranger," refuses to forgive her and vows they must remain apart. *Douglas* was a tragedy written by John Home in 1756.

25. "Drew iron tears down Pluto's cheek," John Milton, "Il Penseroso," line 107. Even Adams, the staid intellectual, confessed in his diary, "I could not resist a few tears," over Fanny Kemble's portrayal of Mrs. Haller at the same performance (CFA *Diary* 5:70).

26. "His form had yet not lost all its original brightness," Milton, *Paradise Lost*, book 1, line 587.

27. Lydia Gray Ward and Thomas Wren Ward, a Boston merchant and treasurer of Harvard University, lived at 3 Park Street.

28. Perhaps the tragedy (1682) by Thomas Otway in which all major characters died was unappealing after the emotionally draining *Fazio* and *The Stranger*.

29. Mary Boardman Crowninshield and her husband, Benjamin, the former secretary of the navy (1815–18), and now a banker and merchant, lived at 1 Somerset Place.

30. *The Gamester* (1753) was a tragedy written by Edward Moore. AQ may be recalling the statement on Kemble in London's *New Monthly Magazine* describing him as possessing "all fire, spirit, and gallantry, mixed with that manly grace and nobility of bearing of which nobody on the stage, except Charles Kemble . . . have any notion." "The Drama," *New Monthly Magazine* 136 (April 1832): 158.

31. The Ladies May Fair held at Faneuil Hall for the benefit of the blind attracted a crowd of about 11,000 and raised more than $12,000 during its four days, 1–4 May. Among the articles for sale were musical compositions and literary works (*Boston Evening Transcript*, 30 April and 6 May 1833; *Boston Morning Post*, 1 May and 4 May 1833).

32. "Possest by wild barbarians fierce in arms," Pope, trans., *Odyssey*, book 6, line 141.

33. George Barrett, a manager at the Tremont Theatre, often acted with his wife in the short pieces that customarily followed the main performance (Clapp, *Record of the Boston Stage*, 298; Notes, 43; Odell, *Annals of the New York Stage*, 3:121, 524).

NOTES TO CHAPTER 3

1. Cushing, "Undergraduate Life Sixty Years Ago," 556–57, Farrar, *The Young Lady's Friend*, 366.

2. Farrar, *The Young Lady's Friend*, 296.

3. Ibid., 390.

4. Notes, 24.

5. Farrar, *The Young Lady's Friend*, 294–95.

6. Probably a reference to a family member; Mrs. H. Keating was a daughter of Hannah Quincy Storer, AQ's great aunt (Storer Family Genealogy, Massachusetts Historical Society).

7. AQ was misled by this apparently cool conversation; later that year Martha Salisbury married Theodore Dwight Woolsey (1801–89), then a professor of Greek at Yale College and later Yale's president (1846–71). She bore him nine children before her death in 1852.

8. Stephen Salisbury (1798–1884), the heir to his father Stephen's Boston importing business and a cousin of Martha Salisbury, married Rebekah Scott Dean (d. 1843) 7 November 1833 (Salisbury, *Family-Memorials*, 35). Robert Burns, "To a Mouse," line 40.

9. AQ later added: "note, 1869 Mr. Chaplain, died in Oct: 1840 on his wedding day! his widow survives to this date."

10. The Botanical Garden, founded in 1805, is the oldest of its kind in the United States. It can be found on the map of Cambridge (see illustration).

11. The Henry Wares, father ("Dr.") and son ("Mr."), usually alternated preaching at the chapel's morning and evening services, occasionally sharing the Sunday services with John Gorham Palfrey (*Eighth Report to Overseers, 1832–1833*, i).

12. Jane Austen, *Mansfield Park* (1814).

13. Convers Francis (1795–1863), a Unitarian clergyman and later professor at Harvard Divinity School, delivered the Dudleian lecture, given each year by a different theologian. Francis's topic was the idolatry of the Roman Catholic Church (Josiah Quincy to Francis, 21 January 1833, Manuscript Collection, Boston Public Library).

14. Sophia Morton was the wife of Eliza Quincy's nephew Robert (AQ travel journal, entry for 3 August 1834).

15. In act 5 of *The Hunchback* (1832) by James S. Knowles, Julia begs the hunchback, Walter (who turns out to be her father), not to force her to marry Lord Rochdale, pleading, "Devise some speedy means to cheat the altar of its victim! Do it!" All ends happily when Julia is allowed to marry her true love, Sir Thomas Clifford.

16. Jane Austen, *Northanger Abbey* (1817).

17. James Alvord had been temporarily appointed to fill the professorship of the recently deceased John Ashmun (*Eighth Report to Overseers, 1832–1833*, xix).

18. Probably the Gilbert Stuart portrait of AQ's grandfather (1744–75), lawyer and patriot. See illustrations, *A Pride of Quincys* (Boston: Massachusetts Historical Society, 1969). AQ recalled that family portraits hung on each side of the parlor door (Notes, 48).

19. "Scenes at the Fair," a satirical sketch attributed to George Parish, was actually written by Fanny Inglis, who ran a Boston boarding school with her family. The pamphlet ridiculed the Faneuil Hall fair, especially Eliza Boardman Otis, who was thinly disguised as "Mrs. Harrowby Grey." Samuel Eliot Morison, *Harrison Gray Otis 1765–1848: The Urbane Federalist* (Boston: Houghton Mifflin, 1969), 491–92.

20. Harriet Beresford Poang Crafts (c. 1774–1839) (Mrs. William), mother of the Harvard undergraduate George Crafts, was visiting from Charleston, S.C. Crafts and Crafts, *A Genealogical and Biographical History*, 187, 189.

21. The first Edmund Quincy (1602–c. 1636), AQ's great-great-great-great grandfather, had come to America in 1633 (genealogical chart, *A Pride of Quincys*).

22. Founded in 1807 as a library, museum, and literary society, the Athenaeum had not permitted women to join until 1829. It was then located at 13 Pearl Street. The annual "Exhibition of Pictures" had opened on 15 May. Jane S. Knowles, "Changing Images of the Boston Athenaeum," in *Change and Continuity: A Pictorial History of the Boston Athenaeum* (Boston: Boston Athenaeum, 1976), 6; *Boston Morning Post*, 19 June 1833, p. 3.

23. Probably a party hosted by Katherine Parks, one of four female members who, along with a number of Harvard professors, founded the Cambridge Book Club in the 1830s. *Cambridge Historical Society Publications* 28 (1942): 112.

24. Possibly adapted from Alexander Pope's "To Lord Bathurst," in *Moral Essays*, Epistle 3, lines 306–8 ("Gallant and gay, in Cliveden's proud alcove").

25. The fight between carpenters working on the new meetinghouse (First Parish Church) and Harvard students originated on the afternoon of 30 May, when a student grabbed a rope involved in the construction and was "insulted" by a workman. Later that evening, when the two met to "settle the affair," students and other workmen joined the struggle. It continued until President Quincy, who happened to be riding by, "put a stop to it" (diaries of Harvard College students Henry Lee and George Moore, 30 May 1833, Harvard University Archives).

NOTES TO CHAPTER 4

1. CFA *Diary*, 21 June 1833, 5:110.

2. Quoted in CFA *Diary* 5:116; see also *Boston Atlas*, 27 June 1833.

3. Harvard Corporation Records, 1833, p. 321; Harvard Overseers' Records, 1833, p. 130, Harvard University Archives; "The President in Boston," *Boston Morning Post*, 24 June 1833, p. 2; Andrew M. Davis, "Jackson's LL.D.—A Tempest in a Teapot," *Massachusetts Historical Society Proceedings*, 2d series, 20 (December 1906): 490–512.

4. *Boston Evening Transcript*, 24 June 1833, p. 2; "Visit of the President to Harvard University," *Boston Courier*, 27 June 1833, p. 2; Edmund Quincy, *Life of Josiah Quincy of Massachusetts* (Boston: Ticknor and Fields, 1867), 454.

5. "Visit of the President," *Boston Courier*, 27 June 1833, p. 2.

6. *Boston Evening Transcript*, 26 June 1833, p. 2.

7. Davis, "Jackson's LL.D.," 494–512; McCaughey, *Josiah Quincy*, 158.

8. Thomas Gray, "Elegy Written in a Country Churchyard," line 56.

9. AQ later added in pencil: "& dressing gowns."

10. Julius Tower (b. 1811) of Waterville, N.Y., married Delia Hearsey in September 1832. Charlemagne Tower, comp., *Tower Genealogy: An Account of the Descendants of John Tower, of Hingham, Mass.* (Cambridge: John Wilson and Son, 1891), 295, 478. Julius's brother Charlemagne (1809–89), about whom the sisters wax so enthusiastic, had graduated from Harvard in 1830 and was then studying law in Waterville. He later became a Harvard Overseer.

11. Several "Maitlands" were prominent in British history. AQ may possibly be thinking of Sir Frederick Lewis Maitland (1777–1839), a naval officer who transported Napoleon after his defeat at Waterloo, or William Maitland (c. 1528–1573), a Scottish politician and defender of Mary Queen of Scots.

12. The hero of Samuel Richardson's *Sir Charles Grandison* (1754), known for his elegant appearance.

13. "Maelzel's Exhibition of the Conflagration of Moscow," depicting Napoleon's 1812 assault on the city, was then being performed nightly at Boston's Exhibition Hall, admission fifty cents. *Boston Morning Post*, 19 June 1833, p. 3.

14. This building is described as a "primitive athletic facility" that Harvard constructed in 1800 on the Charles River near Ash Street. Bunting and Nylander, *Report Four: Old Cambridge*, 156.

15. AQ ends volume 2 of her diary with this inscription. Volume 3 begins with the 16 June entry.

16. "Castle of Indolence" (1748) is a poem by James Thomson.

17. The USS *Constitution*, famed for its victories in the War of 1812, was then being rebuilt.

18. Lewis Cass (1782–1866), then Jackson's secretary of war; Joel Poinsett (1779–1851), a former ambassador to Mexico and a strong Jackson supporter.

19. Shakespeare, *Macbeth*, 5.5.27–28. Presumably a party at the home of Lucretia Goddard Gould, wife of the Boston merchant Benjamin Apthorp Gould, at 5 Winthrop Place.

20. Martin van Buren (1782–1862), vice-president of the United States 1833–37.

21. Joseph Correa Walsh was the brother of Robert Moylan Walsh (1811–72), a diplomat and journalist, and the son of the author Robert Walsh (1784–1859). J. C. Walsh, "Robert Walsh," *Journal of the American Irish Historical Society* 26 (1927), 224.

22. Although the British prevailed in this early Revolutionary War battle of June 1775, they did not capture the heights of Dorchester and Charlestown. A monument to commemorate the battle had been begun in 1825 and was completed in 1843. "Freedom! Yet thy banner, torn, but flying, / Streams like the thunder-storm against the wind," Lord Byron, *Childe Harold's Pilgrimage*, canto 4, stanza 98.

23. "Fore swifter," a nautical term to describe the rope used to keep the capstan bars in place. J. Totten, *Naval Text-Book and Dictionary* (New York: D. Van Nostrand, 1864), 292, 422.

24. At the "Third Grand Concert" held in the Masonic Temple, Signora and Signor Petrotti, Signor Fornasari, and Signor Montresor sang pieces from the operas of Rossini, Bellini, and others (*Boston Evening Transcript*, 25 June 1833, p. 3).

25. George Cabot Davis, the son of Susan Jackson and Isaac P. Davis, had died aboard ship ten days out of Havana (*Boston Courier*, 29 June 1833, p. 2).

NOTES TO CHAPTER 5

1. Daniel M. Wilson, *Three Hundred Years of Quincy, 1625–1925* (Boston: Wright and Potter, 1926), 54, 59; Notes, 2–3.

2. "Our portion is to die . . . " Lord Byron, "Heaven and Earth," line 899.

3. Probably a reference to some close embrace in performances by the French ballet dancers M. and Mme. Ronzi Vestris, who were then touring the United States (Odell, *Annals of the New York Stage*, 3:379, 403).

4. Henry R. Bishop composed this song, with words by Thomas Moore. Helen K. Johnson, *Our Familiar Songs and Those Who Made Them* (New York: Henry Holt, 1909), 515–16.

5. The "Exhibition" in the university chapel consisted of orations in Greek, Latin, and English, along with formal debates and translations, all presented by Harvard's

junior and senior classes. As part of the exhibition, Daniel Webster, then a U.S. senator, gave the annual oration. Unidentified clipping, Harvard University Archives.

6. Robert Bennet Forbes had traveled to China many times in connection with the family's trade with that country. From his fortune acquired in the opium trade he built a house in Milton for his mother, Margaret Perkins Forbes. Phyllis Forbes Kerr, ed., *Letters from China: The Canton-Boston Correspondence of Robert Bennet Forbes* (Mystic, Conn.: Mystic Seaport Museum, 1996), 11–13.

7. "The Peturbed" is Frederick Augustus Whitney (1812–80), a senior at Harvard and son of Peter Whitney, the minister of the First Congregational Church in Quincy. *Memorials of the Class of 1833* (Cambridge: J. Wilson and Son, 1883), 87–88.

8. Psalm 139:9.

9. The Dane Law Building was constructed in 1832 in the Harvard Yard, thanks to a donation from the philanthropist Nathan Dane. It burned in 1918 and was replaced by the present Matthews Hall. Bunting and Nylander, *Report Four: Old Cambridge*, 156–57.

10. AQ later added in pencil in the margin, "ˣDick Fay!!"

11. The First Parish Church (Unitarian), still standing in Harvard Square today, was then being constructed close to the site of the old Fourth Meetinghouse. Bunting and Nylander, *Report Four: Old Cambridge*, 135; *Eighth Report to Overseers, 1832–1833*, 1–2.

12. The phrase "& believe in him" is written in a different color ink; AQ presumably added it later.

13. Perhaps an adaptation from "And conscious Virtue, still its own Reward," from Alexander Pope, trans., *The First Book of Statius His Thebais*, line 758.

14. The exhibit of statues and funeral monuments by pupils of Antonio Canova (1757–1822), recently imported from Italy, had opened at Corinthian Hall at Milk and Federal Streets in Boston, admission twenty-five cents.

15. J. L. Cunningham's auction house, located under Corinthian Hall, was exhibiting a copy of the tomb of the Roman statesman Publius Cornelius Scipio (184?–129? B.C.). *Boston Morning Post*, 1 August 1833, p. 3, 2 August 1833, p. 3. "To what base uses we may return, Horatio!" Shakespeare, *Hamlet*, 5.1.222.

16. Of the miniature cotton manufacture exhibit the *Boston Morning Post* observed that those interested in seeing a factory in progress "can with a trifling expense see and examine the whole operation in the Hall of Industry" ("Hall of Industry," 1 August 1833, p. 2). At Harding's Room a young artist had sculpted the figures from Robert Burns's 1791 poem "Tam o' Shanter. A Tale" ("Tam O'Shanter and Souter Johnny," *Boston Morning Post*, 23 July 1833, p. 2).

17. Possibly a reference to the hymn "Our God Our Help in Ages Past" (1719), by Isaac Watts.

18. *Memoirs of Richard Lovell Edgeworth, esq., begun by himself and concluded by his daughter, Maria Edgeworth* (London: R. Hunter, 1820).

19. Charles Torrigiani visited the Quincys in August along with James Thal of St. Petersburg (*Memoir*, 224).

20. The pretentious Mrs. Elton boasts about riding in this elegant carriage in Jane Austen's *Emma* (vol. 2, chap. 14).

21. AQ added in pencil after "character" the exclamation "oh!" The Harvard summer vacation began on 17 July (*Catalogue of the Officers and Students of Harvard University for the Academical Year 1832–1833*, 23–24).

22. The British-born Edward John Trelawny (1792–1881) had indeed been an adventurer who married a young Greek woman in the 1820s. His friendship with the poets Byron and Shelley had given him a degree of fame, which became more pronounced after the publication of his *Adventures of a Younger Son* (1831), a mixture of half-truths. Coincidentally, while in the United States, Trelawny had traveled with Charles and Fanny Kemble to Niagara Falls in early August. William St. Clair, *Trelawny: the Incurable Romancer* (London: John Murray, 1977), 117, 149, 182–83. In Byron's *Corsair*, Medora, lover of the pirate chief Conrad, dies of grief when she mistakenly hears that Conrad has been killed.

23. The colorful Virginia congressman and senator John Randolph (b. 1773) had died on 24 May. The Boston papers were full of reminiscences of him.

24. In 1803 Thomas Moore had translated poems by the Greek lyric poet Anacreon (c. 570–c. 485 B.C.).

25. Fanny Burney, *Evelina* (1788). AQ later added in the margin, "query— Is this the Mr. G. who has been our Consul at Naples? 1846."

26. Probably the Boston home of Hannah Lee, widow of George G. Lee, at 51 Mt. Vernon St.

27. AQ kept another journal the following year, from 3 to 15 August 1834, when she, her parents, and her sister Abby traveled to New York City and up the Hudson River to visit her mother's family in New Windsor and Malta, N.Y. Filled with conventional descriptions of Hudson River scenery and visits with family, this diary, also in the form of a letter, contrasts with the lively entries of 1833. Did the Harvard environment inspire her animated character sketches, her irony?

AQ's opinions on various subjects are indexed under the name or topic (e.g., Sumner, Charles, or Death). Italics indicate identifications; asterisks indicate tentative identifications.

Index

Index

Index